Furnace of Life
from Nigeria to America

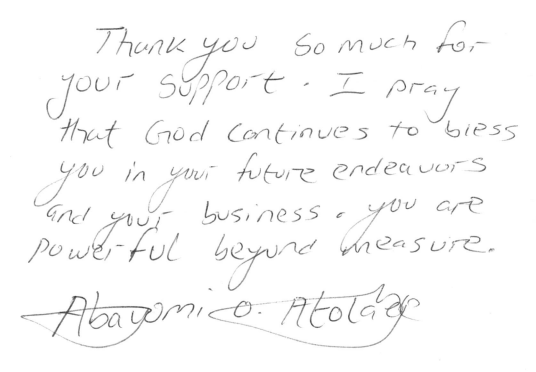

Thank you so much for your support. I pray that God continues to bless you in your future endeavors and your business. You are powerful beyond measure.

Abayomi O. Atolagbe

Abayomi Atolagbe

outskirts
press

Outskirts Press, Inc.
http://www.outskirtspress.com

Paperback ISBN: 978-1-4787-8455-5

PRINTED IN THE UNITED STATES OF AMERICA

TABLE OF CONTENTS

DEDICATION

To my grandmother, Latifat Abeni Kareem, thank you for the valuable discipline and work ethic you instilled in me while growing up in Lagos Island, Lagos Nigeria. They helped me persevere in very tough times over the years. You are a super woman and I pray that God (Allah, Yahweh) continues to keep you strong and keeps your mind sharp for many years to come.

To my mother, Kudirat Kareem, you are a woman who loves God and people very much. People love to be around you and enjoy your joyful spirit, but most have no clue what you have been through over the years. I love you, Mother, and I pray God blesses you with the wonderful desires of your heart and continues to cover you. Thank you for reviewing the book manuscript also.

To my sister, Simisola Atolagbe, I am so proud of the intelligent, strong, beautiful, black woman and leader you are becoming. You are more talented and gifted than you think, and I believe you will do even greater things in your field. I like that you love to honor Yahweh. I pray Yahweh continues to order your steps and bless you with the good desires of your heart. Thank you for reviewing the book manuscript too.

To the Urban League Young Professionals of Middle TN (ULYPMT) executive committee of 2014-2016, I appreciate your time and effort in helping to serve the Nashville, TN community and surrounding places to make peoples' lives a little bit better in the areas of jobs, education, healthy lifestyle, housing affordability, and youth empowerment.

Thank you VP Briana Johnson Moore, Treasurer and Economic Empowerment Chair Barrington Gist, Secretary Shani Glapion, Policy and Procedures Chair Erin Lynch Alexander, Membership Chair Nekeia Booker, Community and Civic Engagement Chair Jonathan Adair, Youth Advocacy Chair Robert Robinson, Fund Raising Chair Lane Marks, Health Advocacy Chair Teka Moten, Communications Chair Ivy Johnson, Communications Co – Chairs Lydia Dumas and Taz Crawford, Membership Co- Chairs Cassanora Lamply and Narja McElroy, and Policy and Procedures Chair Mariah Cole. Thank you.

FOREWORD

The House of Alpha
Brother Sydney P. Brown

Goodwill is the monarch of this house, men
Unacquainted, enter, shake hands, exchange
Greetings and depart friends. Cordiality exists
Among all who abide within. I am the eminent
Expression of friendship. Character and
Temperament change under my dominant power.
Lives once touched by me become tuned and are
Thereafter amiable, kindly, fraternal.
I inspire the musician to play noble sentiments and
Assist the chemist to convert ungenerous
Personalities into individuals of great worth.
I destroy ignoble impulses. I constantly invoke
Principles which make for common brotherhood
And the echo resounds in all communities and
Princely men are thereby recognized. Education,
Health, music, encouragement, sympathy, laughter:
All these are species of interest given of self-
Invested capital.

Tired moments find me a delightful treat, hours of
Sorrow, a shrine of understanding, at all times I am
Faithful to the creed of companionship, to a few,
I Am the castle of dreams, ambitious, successful,
Hopeful dreams. To many, I am the poetic place
Where human feeling is rhymed to celestial
Motives; to the great majority, I am the treasury of
Good fellowship.
In fact, I am the college of friendship; the
University of brotherly love; the school for the
Better making of men.

I AM ALPHA PHI ALPHA!

ACKNOWLEDGEMENT

FURNACE OF LIFE: From Nigeria to America is Providence, not coincidence. I acknowledge God (Yahweh, Allah) for entrusting and allowing me to live a life that has positively impacted many others and will continue to do so. I am thankful to God for blessing me with the strength, patience, spirit, courage, tenacity, endurance, grit, protection, grace, and mercy to walk this path. I am thankful to share my life story with others. Ladies and gentlemen, it has not been easy, and one of the traits I learned from my mother is the ability to function well, perform, and smile whenever I have to go through the furnace. I also thank my mother for encouraging me to write about the pain and obstacles regarding my journey in life and career.

To London Thomas, the artist who helped enhanced the custom art I drew to capture the theme for the book and who helped me make it come to life by adding colors to it, thank you so much. I wish you success in your future endeavors. Stay cool.

To Dennie Marshall, Shawn Modena, William Hytche, and Barrington Gist, thank you for taking the time and sending the book statements I requested. You all are a very good example of what it means to be a man, a leader, and a friend.

To Mrs. Karla Davis, I appreciate you for reviewing the book. Despite your busy schedule, you took the time to go over the book manuscript and communicated areas of improvement to me. Thank you so much for keeping it real with me, suggesting an editor, and telling it like it is to help make sure the book is ready for the public.

To Amani Murph and Edwina Onofua, you are true friends that a friend can rely on. You volunteered to help me speak to people about the book for my first book signing and read the book manuscript to prepare. Glad I met you both and I hope you get blessed with the wonderful desires of your heart.

PREFACE

THERE WAS A point I did not want to continue writing this book, but my heart could not rest. Days, weeks, months, even years went by with the book on pause due to challenges at my job, life, and faith. However, an inner voice constantly reminded me that I needed to write about it and finish this book. It is like it was meant to be written. When I resumed writing, peace resumed within me. There were times when I questioned why I was putting my life and experiences out in the public's eye. Even a friend asked if I was concerned about what people will think of me and how the world will view my family and relatives. Even prior to the question, I thought about those things and they kept me from wanting to finish the book. However, the unrest I experienced while the book was on hold was stronger. The furnace of life, which is my collection of experiences from Nigeria and America, is nothing to be ashamed of. It is the opposite. It demonstrates how young men and young women can overcome the odds and do successful things in life, despite the circumstances of upbringing and obstacles.

This book is God inspired. It is a story that required me to be very transparent, honest, and candid about my life. It matters not if some people look down on me or think negatively of me. What matters is that I obeyed God (Yahweh, Allah). Usually, the ones who do great things in life and positively impact other lives—whether in areas of engineering, technology, medicine, sport, research study, music, movie, art, business, or love—are not limited by what people think. They dare to shatter the box of fear that keeps too many from fulfilling their purpose in life and being truly joyful and happy. To truly make an impact on this earth, it requires honesty, a strong work ethic, and an authentic spirit. No one is perfect. I believe real changes and good solutions to most of the problems on this earth will only occur when we start being honest with each other in words and actions. An authentic person is more relatable in the eyes of the majority. It pays to be real (honest) in a world full of deception and deceivers who claim to be good but are nothing but pretenders. I do not fully understand God's approach, but I have no doubt that the purpose of this book is beyond me. It is about the many lives that will be healed and positively influenced with this book. It is a voice for the timid to use courage, let go of the hurt, communicate about it, act, overcome any obstacle, choose to be happy, realize their potential, and dare to take that leap of faith even as eagles must do to soar.

Furnace of Life: from Nigeria to America is a very good read and will keep you curious, laughing at times, and wondering what will happen next. It is a tool that gets the conversation going, bringing to light childhood and adulthood experiences-struggles by both females and males that we (parents-children) too often keep quiet about due to fear or shame. It provides workable solutions for young men, women, and adults that are going through or may go through similar experience(s) detailed in book. It will positively influence lives on an international scale because it required me to let my guards down, ask questions, and be as transparent as possible to be a part of the positive (real) change on this earth. The book focuses on seven areas.

1. It details my life experiences in Lagos Island (Lagos, Nigeria) and in the United States of America, from primary school, secondary school (high school), college life, and professional life.
2. The life experiences include overcoming being molested as a

child from the age of 10 to 11 by an older female relative and my struggles as a child. It details the love, care, and discipline of my grandmother who raised me, transition to and experiences in America, being homeless, multiple rejections and lengthy delays in my career endeavors, my choice to remain celibate till the age of 29 and reasons behind it, and how I overcame the hardships and obstacles of life, while staying involved in the community, putting myself through high school, college, graduate school, and working in the government and engineering field.

3. It asks the tough questions regarding faith-religion, God, government, career, relationship, intimacy, and exposes a clever system of inequality.

4. It details my failures, common to both males and females, triumphs, how to handle rejections-failures, and why they are like a foundation for any level of success.

5. It explains how my parents' divorce affected me as a boy and a young man, why a son can hate his dad for abusing his mom, and how I forgave and overcame not having a father around.

6. It details a study of Lagos, Nigeria (people, government, environment, and the economic and living conditions) after not being back home in 20 years since I came with my mother and sister to America at the age of 13. It also shows my love for both Nigeria (country of birth) and its culture, my love for United States of America, the good-bad-ugly conditions in both countries, and ideas on how to engender a community to help make people's lives a little bit better.

7. The book has valuable lessons of life and anyone can benefit from it no matter if you are an adult, young, president, teacher, lawyer, janitor, governor, doctor, nurse, athlete, coach, gangster, republican, democrat, business man or business woman, drug dealer, saint, sinner, judge, prostitute, preacher, stripper, accountant, engineer, mayor, council member, Muslim,

Christian, Jew, Buddhist, lesbian, gay, scientist, or an entertainer. No matter your background or affiliation, the book has something for you to gain or share with a loved one. It is providence, not coincidence.

Abayomi Oluwaseun Abdulmajid Samuel Atolagbe
info@moortech.org
aba_eli@yahoo.com
United States of America

Chapter 1
Memories, Childhood – Lagos Island (Lagos, Nigeria)

My FIRST MEMORY of existing on Earth dated back to a moment my mother, Kudirat Kareem, held me in her arms. She is a beautiful, outgoing, and caring woman who likes to laugh a lot. I also remember running on the second floor of a four-story building I grew up in. I loved to run as a child. At the age of seven, with a curiosity for airplanes, I ran and jumped off staircases for fun. The thrill of flight was second to none. My grandmother, Latifat Abeni Kareem, raised me, my sister, and our cousins in a building located on 15 Forsythe Street, Lafiaji, Lagos Island, Lagos, Nigeria. My mother worked at a Nigerian telecommunications company (NITEL) and lived in Ibadan, Nigeria. My dad moved to United States of America when I was three years old. I looked forward to every visit to see my mother in Ibadan. My mother's friends, church members, and neighbors loved me and took care of me when mom was at work. On occasions, mom took me to her job at NITEL. She was a very good data entry specialist. Mom also visited Lagos often and made sure she provided my grandmother with the money to cover the expenses to help raise my sister and me.

Grandmother helped raised the six children of her two daughters: my mother and her big sister Toyin, known as Sisimi. Sisimi's children are Saidat, Bolaji, Kemi, and Bisi. My biological sister's name is Simisola. The children of my grandmother's two sons visited Forsythe often. The ones I remember are Moyo, Rasak, Rasheed, and Oyin. Grandmother was a businesswoman, tall, strong, good communicator, and made sure her grandchildren are disciplined and worked hard. Although she was strict, she was very loving too. She was a tailor and trained many tailors. She also sold dry food items, hygiene products, alcohol and non-alcoholic drinks, cigarettes, water, and all types of toys and items to celebrate Nigerian Independence Day, Christmas, and New Year. She also sold sugar, matches, candy, and medicine. Forsythe Street had a lot of commerce and transactions of goods and services. Most of the businesses on a quarter of Forsythe Street were auto parts shops. Forsythe Street was at least one mile long.

My grandmother is a true super woman and a Muslim. She loved to observe the annual Muslim holiday (Ramadan). It is a very important time in the Muslim faith and known as the period Allah (God) revealed the Koran to Prophet Mohammad. Muslims also fast from sunrise to sunset during this period. She also enjoys to get the entire family together annually to celebrate family. She purchased the best ram available in the market and all types of food to eat during this period. The annual gathering of the entire family is like America's annual Thanksgiving holiday. Baba Moyo, one of my grandmother's sons, a panel beater (repairs a vehicle body after damage) by profession, and a boxer was known for his dedication for conducting the complex and long process of preparing a ram every year before grandmother's daughters and two daughter-in-laws started to cook. Two popular games occurred annually when the rams were still living and after the rams were slaughtered. I remember the young and the old gathering together to watch living rams fight each other by colliding horns. The rams would back up to get enough distance, and then they sprinted towards each other to have the power necessary during impact (colliding horns at full speed.) The weak ram eventually stopped fighting. After the rams were slaughtered, many young boys like me could not wait to get our hands on the horns of the rams. We heated the horns in firewood and collided them with concrete or a tree with just enough impact. This impact is what helped to gradually remove everything inside the horns. We then put sticks or iron rods in the horns. Children gathered together and collided the horns for fun. The stick or iron rod was held while colliding the horns. The horn that came out of a stick or iron first lost the game. Winning felt good.

Growing up in Forsythe was a lot of fun and a lot of hard work. My cousins, sister, and I walked miles sometimes to fetch water, carried crates of drinks home on our head from Coca-Cola trucks, and conducted other housework. I loved proving and hearing Grandmother comment me on my strength. Sometimes, we took a bus to the market to shop with Grandmother. We walked in very congested areas filled with motorcycle noises, taxicabs, and different types of people: rich, poor, thugs, beggars, blind, lame, traders, sellers, buyers, thieves, and policemen. At the age of 11, I started going to the market alone to get products for Grandmother as needed. On occasions, I took the bus to the market, walked miles back with the products on a very busy bridge, and spent the money Grandmother gave me for transportation back home on food or snacks. One day, I got caught. I experienced one of the worst beatings of my life. Speaking of discipline and beatings, grandmother was known to use belts, canes, and wires to correct us when we acted bad or failed to do something. The beatings included going into a room, taking off our clothes sometimes, and getting flogged with round after round of belt, canes, or wires. Grandmother eventually got tired of beating us and turned the task over to Aunty Saidat. Her beating was even more feared than Grandmother's. She ran and beat at the same time. She was a very cool aunty though. Aunty Kemi loved to read. Uncle Bolaji loved to ride bicycles and go out a lot. Bisi and Simisola sometimes played with other neighborhood kids. Grandmother's and Aunty Saidat's discipline, although could be severe, had a good affect on us because it taught us valuable lessons like responsibility and obedience. The beatings stopped eventually.

We were also very educated. Aunty Kemi, Aunty Saidat, and Uncle Bolaji often left Forsythe for boarding school. Bisi, Simisola, and I looked forward to their return when they came back from school breaks. Bisi went to a nearby school. Simisola and I attended a private school, not far from Forsythe. The name was Abimbola Day Nursery and Primary School. I loved and still miss those days. I had many friends whose faces and names I still remember. I appreciated and respected my teachers. My school trips, sports, activities, debates, spelling contests, and recess activities were very fun. The school's food was usually good. My favorite food was jolof rice, chicken, fried rice, plantains, fish, fruits, yams, and beans. I enjoyed my friends and classmates so much. We played, laughed, cried, and celebrated birthdays constantly. Every single birthday was a special and delightful day. The boys loved to have fun when teachers are not around. Our favorite things to do included wrestling coins off the table to win money, talking with the girls, playing soccer, and joking. The girls loved us too. We had so much fun! I hope to see some of my friends again in the future.

I had a childhood crush at the school. I had dreams about her while growing up in Nigeria and on occasions in United States of America. I have even tried to connect with her on FaceBook, but I can't find her profile. She is probably married now. She was very intelligent, beautiful, tall, and had a short natural hairstyle. She has an older sister and a younger brother. Her mother was very nice. One of her friends liked to joke a lot about my childhood crush and I as a future couple. This friend was very energetic and funny. I liked talking to my childhood crush and sitting by her. I smiled and wondered about her a lot. I pray to God that my classmates and friends are safe wherever they are and happy with whomever they are with.

After primary school, I attended a public school called Eko Akete; the school was a few miles from home. My two fun memories about that school were playing soccer during recess and occasionally crossing paths with my childhood crush on my way back home after school. She attended Holy Child (school for girls). Walking to and from school was very common in Lagos, Nigeria. Some children traveled by car or bus, or parents came to pick them up depending on the distance. After leaving Eko Akete, I attended Ibadan Grammar School and eventually stayed in what was called a dormitory back then. I did not like Eko Akete. It was underfunded and had low standards. Classrooms were in bad shape. It was noisy. At Ibadan Grammar school, some senior students were mean (especially the dormitory seniors). They considered new residents as inferior. They claimed the bottom bunk bed. They sometimes took our food, cereal, chocolate milk, snacks, toothpaste, detergents, etc. Some made us wash their laundry. All the new students and residents were isolated and helpless because we just could not confront the seniors. Telling the headmaster (dormitory director) was useless. The environment itself was dangerous at times. We often came across different types of snakes because the dormitory was built in a rural area, very close to nature. Thugs with axes and knives occasionally came to the school hall compound to start trouble. However, one senior gained my respect at Ibadan Grammar School. His nickname was Nator. He was not mean, but was well respected. He was often called on to help kill snakes, and he led other residents to confront the thugs. Nator was tall and fearless. He taught me to have no fear. Eventually, I moved back to Lagos to live with Grandmother prior to coming to America at the age of thirteen.

Chapter 2
MISTAKES, CHILDHOOD –
LAGOS ISLAND (LAGOS, NIGERIA)

LOOKING BACK AT my life as a young boy growing up in Forsythe, I made a few childhood mistakes. I stole and lied at times. I stopped those bad habits at age twelve. I am sure many of my friends, co- workers, and those who know me personally in America will have a hard time picturing me stealing or lying. The fact is, as a child, I stole money from Grandmother. Although I regret my mistakes, I laugh when I reminisce, picturing myself as a child secretly drinking my favorite beverage (orange Fanta) or taking out five, ten, and sometimes 20 Naira out of the money basket, rolling it up, and putting it in my school uniform undetected. I purchased snacks like meat pie, chicken pie, and chin chin on my way to school with the money.

To fast forward to when I attended college in America, one of my college roommates used my college I.D. and stole a lot of money from me. I caught another college roommate using my electric shaver without permission. Several people borrowed money from me and never returned it. I was able to forgive because I understood that I made those mistakes as a child.

I had a childhood habit of going to the kitchen, when Grandmother and Aunty were not watching, to take out and eat freshly cooked fish or meat from the soup pot. I do not remember Grandmother or Aunty catching me stealing money, secretly drinking Fanta, or treating myself to tasty meat or fish from the soup pot. However, I remember one of the worst beatings I experienced by Aunty Saidat. It was in the evening time at Forsythe. I recalled being in a room on the second floor, and Aunty Saidat just beat me with a cane for so long that several parts of my body from head to toe swelled instantly. She felt bad after the fact and embraced me. That did not help the bruises and swelling, though.

Eventually, a positive change in character from bad (ages 7 – 12) to good (ages 12 – 28) was made. I will reveal another phase I call good to real (ages 28 - up). The fact is the discipline of my grandmother and aunty influenced me positively. My mother's struggle after my sister, mother, and I moved to America when I was thirteen years old, being homeless after just months of us living with dad, and eventually in custody of the state of Tennessee living in the shelter for a while due to Dad abusing Mom made me determined to break the cycle and strive for better days. This is the secret and reason behind why I am so gentle and honest, why I've persevered, and why I strive to not disrespect women emotionally or physically. This is the reason I work hard, barely act negatively on anger, and stay very humble. This is the reason I can be very quiet at times. My life struggles and the rejections I experienced in my career endeavors literally molded me. I don't like to talk much. I will rather act. Life made me. I am literally raised by life and I'm a radical for truth. I am neither limited by faith nor influenced by evil. I am a fearless and limitless soul. I read the entire Bible when I was in high school. Jesus Christ's examples and his command to love people is the building block of my character. I struggled with my Christian faith, which will be revealed a few chapters from now. Anyway, the type of love I am referring to sums up the will of God and any true faith. The Apostle Paul said,

If I speak in the tongues of men and of angels, but have not love, I am only a resounding gong or a clanging cymbal. If I have the gift of prophecy and can fathom all mysteries and all knowledge, and if I have a faith that can move mountains, but have not love, I am nothing. If I

give all I possess to the poor and surrender my body to be burned by the flames, but have not love, I gain nothing. Love is patient. Love is kind. It does not envy. It does not boast. It is not proud. It is not rude. It is not self-seeking. It is not easily angered. It keeps no record of wrongs. Love does not delight in evil but rejoices with the truth. It always protects, always trusts, always hopes, always perseveres. Love never fails. But where there are prophecies, they will cease; where there are tongues, they will be stilled; where there is knowledge, it will pass away. For we know in part and we prophesy in part, but when perfection comes, the imperfect disappears. When I was a child, I talked like a child. I thought like a child. I reasoned like a child. When I became a man, I put away childish things. For now, we see only a reflection as in a mirror; then we shall see face to face. Now I know in part; then I shall know fully, even as I am fully known. And now these three remain: faith, hope and love. But the greatest of these is love. (I Corinthians. 13. 1-13, NIV version)

Chapter 3
COMING TO AMERICA, CHILDHOOD – NASHVILLE, TN

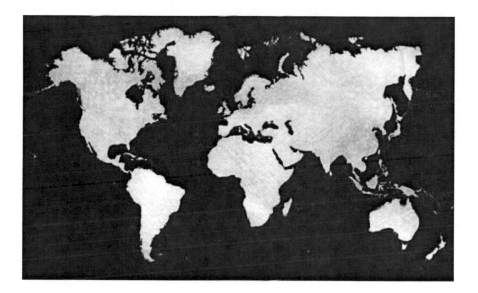

THE WORDS "U.S. embassy. We are going to America" still cause me to reflect sometimes. After a second attempt by my dad to bring my sister, Mom, and I to the United States of America to live and continue school, it was approved. Mixed emotions kicked in because I had not seen my classmates and friends in a while. Now I would be separated from them. At the same time, my thirteen-year-old perception of America kept me happy. Little did I know that going to America would begin close to two decades of the experience I call the "furnace of life." I have been tested in the furnace and it has made me exponentially stronger, giving me a golden heart, a wise mind, and a soul to serve. I am allergic to anyone or anything counterfeit and evil. Think twice before approaching me. I love everything that's genuine and have zero tolerance for evil and bullshit.

It seemed like yesterday that my mom, sister, and I left Forsythe for America after saying our goodbyes to family. I remember being at the airport filled with amazement regarding how nice the interior looked, the colors, people, and the type of technology it had. It felt like my life was getting ready to change. No more hard work? No more walking long distances at times? No more heat? To my surprise, I was wrong.

We finally entered what I have always looked at with amazement in the sky for years: an airplane, a symbol of the unrealistic turned into reality. Even to this day, an airplane is a symbol and reminder to me that anything is possible if we do not give up on our goals and aspirations. I am sure the Wright Brothers who were the first in flight will agree. If humans can design and engineer airplanes that can get over 80 meters long and around 5 meters wide, with the ability to carry over 500 people comfortably from one country to another in mid air, I believe anything is possible. Of course, the forces of flight (gravity, lift, thrust, and drag) make this possible with the help of powerful engines. It is just awesome that humans are blessed with such a capability. We stopped in Amsterdam, caught another airplane to Detroit, Michigan, before we arrived in Nashville, TN. The experience and food was worth the trip. We arrived at the Nashville airport in the winter of 1996; Dad came to pick us up. After we settled in his two-bedroom apartment in Elm Hill Pike and ate, one of the things that caught my attention was a picture of Dr. Martin Luther King Jr. and his "I Have a Dream" speech mounted on the wall of the living room. My sister and I shared a room with two beds.

As expected after we arrived in America, many Nigerians and Americans came to visit us. Dad also took us to Opryland amusement park, on several visits to his friends, and to an all-Nigerian organization meeting and social called Egbe Omo Odudua to meet our peers. Dad had many close women friends in America. Prior to my mom, sister, and I coming to America, Dad was in a relationship and had another child with a woman in America. My stepbrother and his mom had moved to Alabama prior to our arrival. Another woman, I'll call her Woman Two, was in Nashville. Her daughter was not my dad's, however.

Woman Two was a nice person in my mind at the time. She bought me my first pair of green and white Nikes. In fact, Mom, Simisola, Dad, and I visited her often at her house. Keep in mind we had no clue about the level of relationship between Woman Two and my dad. She was a widow. Her daughter and I competed constantly with the game Mario Cart. She and her daughter visited us too. Eventually, my mother and sister stopped visiting her. I am sure my mom eventually noticed something out of order between Woman Two and my dad. I chose to go with Dad. I was fond of the game Mario Cart, liked to ride in Dad's red Mitsubishi Eclipse, and just needed to get out of the apartment when the opportunity allowed. It did not take me long as a thirteen-year-old to discover dad was intimately involved with several women. Woman Three was also in Nashville. She had a son (not my dad's). The son was very fond of me to my amazement. I never saw or met his dad. Eventually, I stopped going with dad to his female friends' houses. I became hateful of dad around this time. Dad eventually had another son with Woman Four, and she moved with my second stepbrother to California. I found out about Woman Five in later years. I eventually stopped counting. So, I have one sister by my dad and mom. I also have two stepbrothers that I am aware of. My dad's infidelities contributed to arguments between him and Mom and eventually led to their divorce as well as to my suspicions about whether he ever loved her.

Chapter 4
LIVING IN AMERICA,
FURNACE OF LIFE – NASHVILLE, TN

,

BEFORE MY MOM and dad divorced, my sister, mom, and I only stayed with him for a few months in America. I started attending Two Rivers Middle School. My mother started work at the nearby Hardee's, about a mile walk from Dad's apartment. Things became bad between Dad and Mom. My sister and I witnessed firsthand what a dangerous, immoral, and abusive relationship looked like.

In addition to attending Lipscomb University for a master's degree, dad was a natural collector and decorator. His apartment had several types of fine arts, drawings, objects, and sculptures from Africa and America. I remember sculptures of different tribes in Lagos, Nigeria. He also had carved animals and multi colored paintings. The statute of the golden lions he had stood out to me. He also had a special Coo Coo clock in the living room, with a carved bird that comes out of the clock often. That bird's noise (Coo Coo..Coo Coo...) was funny to me as a child.

I remember constant late-night arguments and threats between my parents. It was not long before Simisola and I realized that Dad was abusing mom emotionally and physically. Things got worse. I am thankful that my mother is still alive and did not suffer long term emotional trauma with everything I saw her go through.

I recalled countless times when Mom, Simisola, and I watched TV in the living room. Dad brought one of his female friends to the apartment and eventually took her into his bedroom. This happened a few times. I hated his actions, direct disrespect to my mother, and misuse of women. It was a matter of immorality. Those who know me personally and those who have read this far into this book should have a clear hint by now why I have such a deep conviction to respect women. Why it took me so long to even consider dating. Why I treated those women that were attracted to me like a sister. My experience at home was also a part of the reason I waited for so long before being intimate with a woman. I became intimate at the age of twenty-nine. Yes, I battled with several types of temptations. Yes, I thought about having sex a lot and did not. I could have had girlfriends in high school and many in college, but I chose neither to be in a relationship nor be intimate for many years. It is personal. I must break the cycle of violence of all types against women, starting with me. As I am writing this book, currently at twenty-nine years old, I will love for my first girlfriend to be the one I marry. Not sure if that will happen due to reasons in a later chapter. My goals are to be a faithful husband, best friend, provider, protector, and true companion to whoever becomes my wife, and to be a good father to my future children. I constantly remind myself and pray to not be an abusive father or husband.

I mentioned earlier that I attended Two Rivers Middle School. Unfortunately, it was common then for some classmates to make fun of foreign students. I guess it is out of ignorance or due to the habit of some American news stations to mislead its people by portraying Africa as a jungle or uncivilized. Those news stations are deceivers and too often capitalize on negative news to maximize number of viewers. The truth is every country and continent on Earth has its wealthy, rich, middle class, and poor people and places. I constantly heard jokes about how I dressed and spoke as well as ignorant statements about Africa, like how we chased lions and monkeys and ran around naked. They had no clue I came from a big family, with businessmen and businesswomen, and that I was very proud of my Nigerian culture. I don't fault them directly. They were young, childish, and ill-informed about both my heritage and the continent of Africa.

Africa is not actually the original name. The original name is Alkebulan, a place where civilization started. Egypt is in Alkebulan and there were thousands of dynasties beyond Egypt that originated in Alkebulan and pre-dated Christianity. Many forms and styles of castle like and sophisticated way of building originated in Alkebulan. The Moors came from Alkebulan and it is the origin of black kingdoms and ancestors that invented the wheel, classical music and instruments, many types of medicine and forms of healing, writing, the clock, and all types of inventions in modern day era that Western history for some reason do not teach in high school, keeps hidden, and barely makes available at libraries. Some of the Moors, black men (and women), settled in Cordova, Spain in 711 AD. They invented and had profound impact on most of the inventions and technology in civilization today. They influenced Europe, Asia, North America, and South America. They were expert Builders, Alchemists, Architects, Masons, Philosophers, Teachers, Scientists, Mathematicians, Physicists, Astronomers, Astrologists, Classical Musicians, Inventors, Innovators, and Trend Setters. The first university is Europe was started and built by the Moors and many well-known physicists and scientists learned from the Moors. The Moors helped Europe to recover when Europe was going through the dark ages. They raised sidewalks, lighted streets, brought in medicine, soaps, helped to run hot and cold water lines, and just improved the standard of living and health conditions in Europe. It is a matter of research, if you are of "African" descent to know who you truly are and where you came from. Do not let anyone lie to you, make you ignorant, or make you think you are inferior and your history started with slavery. This type of history is a lie. Know thyself, get the facts, and enlighten all people. There are books out there about the origin of civilization, the Moors, and it is a matter of a using some effort to get them. There are also documentaries like Hidden Colors (Part 1, 2, and 3) available to watch.

While attending Two Rivers Middle School, there was a classmate by the name of Robyn who wasn't ignorant. She smiled, spoke with me often, was polite, with a very beautiful spirit.

Things did not get any better at home. My sister got very sick to the point that she had to stay at the hospital for a while. I remember constant visits to the General Hospital in downtown, Nashville, TN. One night, my parents and a male friend of my dad took me to visit my sister at the hospital. As we were leaving, Mom and Dad began to argue. Within moments, Dad physically abused her in front of his male friend and me. It was that night when my hatred for my father's actions grew stronger within me. Moving forward, I was beaten by Dad before he went to work one morning. I don't remember what I did. I just remember getting angry. Eventually during that period, policemen came to Dad's apartment and took Mom and me to the police station. Afterward, we were transported to the shelter and separated from Dad. My sister was still at the hospital. I continued to attend Two Rivers Middle School and woke up early every morning to take the city bus from the shelter to school.

The shelter was very close to the Cabana restaurant. My sister was still in the hospital. I remember Mom would get up for work very early and arrive back at the shelter very late at times. She had no personal vehicle; so, she walked many miles to work for a while. She later started taking the bus, which helped shorten her trip. Life at the shelter wasn't good. Food was scarce. Sometimes the food supply ran out and we would go hungry. I remembered that the weight of the burden on her put her in tears at times. Even at the age of thirteen, I understood the severity of our condition, and it kept me focused, hungry for success in school and life. Although it was rough at the shelter, I did made friends with a set of twins around my age. The shelter had rules, and I made sure I behaved. Children shared rooms. Women shared rooms. We all shared restrooms and living rooms. Privacy was very limited. Outside of school, after completing my homework, my only getaways were shooting basketball and listening to music. Sometimes I played basketball with the twins and another boy a little younger than me. I remember watching the movie Space Jam with them too.

Before I started playing sports in high school, music was my temporary break from the furnace of life. I have a natural talent to pick good music. My familiarity with all types of music started around the time my mom, sister, and I were still living with dad. I woke up to a light rock radio station (Mix 92.9) every morning before getting ready for school. I listened to TLC, Black Street, OutKast, Boyz II Men, and Aaliyah. I loved Michael Jackson's *Dangerous* album. I listen to Mix 92.9 to this day. My favorite vocalists are Celine Dion, Phil Collins, Maxwell, Bryan Adams, Whitney Houston, Aaron Neville, and Lee Ann Womack, just to name a few. Celine Dion's voice is just angelic. I like songs by the groups Creed and Savage Garden. I also watched Rap City, a show on BET, and became familiar with artists like 2Pac, Dr. Dre, Biggie Smalls, Sean "Puffy" Combs, and Masc. Let me briefly call out my sister for her fondness of Backstreet Boys and 'N Sync. She listened to these two groups so much when we were young I had no choice but to listen to them too. I also listened to Jay Z, 50 Cent, Eminem, and gospel rappers Knine and Lecrae. I like Alicia Keys' all-around talent, Keisha Cole's real songs, Mary J. Blige and Lauryn Hill's pure and unique vibe, Monica and KC and Jojo's soulful delivery, R Kelly's natural ability to write deep songs and sing well, and Usher combination of dance and music. Friends, you are probably surprised I said Usher. I have a secret talent for dancing. My mom saw me dance a lot and mimic Michael Jackson as a child.

Speaking of the world's biggest stars, Beyonce is one I didn't like until I watched the movie called *Obsessed*. Her character showed a good example of a strong woman, and her performance turned me into a fan of hers. I eventually added musicians like John Legend and Musiq Soulchild to the list.

Seventeen years later, after earning my engineering degree and Master degree, I started listening to Nigerian musicians like Tiwa Savage, Korede Belo, Q dot, Yemi Alade, Dr. Sid, Wiz Kid, Tekno, P

Square, Olamide, Kiss Daniel, MC Galaxy, Flavour, Davido, Brymo, Adekunle Gold, 2 face, and Bracket. Most of the new school Nigerian musicians mix English and Yoruba in their lyrics. In Nigeria, I grew up hearing traditional musicians who usually sang in the Yoruba language, like Salawa Abeni, King Sunny Ade, Ayinde Barrister, Wasiu Ayinde, Sir Shina Peters, Kollington Ayinla, Obesere, and Fela Kuti (Fela's lyrics are sometimes in broken English). My favorite TV shows in middle school to high school included *Family Matters, Xena: Warrior Princess, Hercules, Fresh Prince of Bel Air, Saved by The Bell,* and *In the Heat of The Night.*

Before we left the shelter, mom met a friend when I was still thirteen years old. They both worked at McKendree Village Health Center in Hermitage, TN. The friend invited us to stay with her family, which included her husband and daughter. The daughter was kind. She shared her bedroom with me and Simisola, who had finally gotten out of the hospital. I played volleyball and ran around with other young boys in the neighborhood for leisure.

In 1997, we moved to Jackson Grove apartments; it was called Hermitage Hills before getting renovated. Mother still walked to McKendree Village, about two miles from our two-bedroom apartment. At the age of fourteen years old, I attended McGavock Comprehensive High School. My sister attended Dupont Tyler Middle School. I was reunited in high school with some of the Two Rivers Middle School classmates that made fun of me. This time around, I was taller, stronger, and unfortunately kept to myself a lot. They did not make fun of me anymore. However, I was hurting inside. I was overwhelmed with being the man of the house, with no father figure around, and knew I had to do whatever I could to protect mom and sister. I struggled with this. My sister and I argued sometimes at home back then over things like TV remote and food. I loved to eat and often go for second and third plates. Luckily, I also liked and still like exercising a lot. I did get in a lot of fights at school, got put out of class a few times, and spent hours at in-school suspension. My mom was fed up with me. I was fed up with life. I chose to move out and go stay with my dad temporarily.

Staying with Dad gave me a little space. I had my own room. That was the only positive thing about it. I thought about my mom and sister a lot and stayed in communication with both. Eventually my sister started attending McGavock High School. After school, each day, I went home to relax. Dad normally returned home at night. I had to iron his clothes, do the laundry, clean the restrooms, keep the apartment in order, shine his shoes, prepare his food, wash the dishes, and more. The interesting thing is these chores were not what complicated things. I did much more in Nigeria. The difference is I was unhappy in America due to the life I was exposed to. I witnessed Dad bringing woman after woman to the apartment. Eventually, they ended up in his bedroom. I remained calm, but this didn't last.

At Dad's apartment, some of the movies and TV channels available to watch had nudity in them. However, my desire to break the cycle was stronger than what I was exposed to constantly. Although I thought about sex at times, I just would not approach a woman with sexual motives in mind. I never even considered dating until I turned twenty-seven years old. I had many friends. I treated the females like sisters and my few friends that were male like brothers. I was known as the "good" guy. It got to a point in my teenage years that I told myself I was not going to marry. The truth was I was afraid of replicating Dad's mistakes.

One night, my dad brought another woman to the apartment. After they left, I was furious. That day, I just started punching the apartment walls. I damaged some objects and punched holes through the walls. When Dad came back home, I did not know how to tell him I was angry. I told him I stumbled several times, damaging the wall and objects. A few days later, another woman came to visit Dad in the morning. The woman could tell I was angry. She left eventually. Dad and I got into an argument. He threatened to put me out of the apartment. He did. I did not care. I exited the apartment after he said get out. He later called me back inside. That did not change my intention to stop living with him. I was ready to leave that place. Something in my spirit convinced me to leave, to separate from the negative lifestyle I was exposed to. I had started to read the Bible on my own by then. I eventually read the entire Bible that period in my life.

One day I called Mom and told her I wanted to come back to live with her. By that time, she had found out that one of my aunties (Ola Adeyemo) and uncles (Ishmael Adeyemo) lived in Antioch, Tennessee. My aunty asked me why I wanted to live with Mom again; so, I told her and Mom why. By the beginning of my junior year in high school, I moved back in with my mom and sister. I made a good decision. I did a lot of self-examination as a junior. From that point on, I became a son any mother would love to have, a brother any sister would love to have, the student any teacher would love to have in a class, and a friend any friend would love to call a friend. My standard was so high academically, socially, physically, and spiritually. I remember telling Mom one time that I didn't want to marry (still shocking to me that I felt that way in high school). I wanted to be like the Apostle Paul at the time. I earned mostly As and a few Bs in school. I joined the football team, was the brightest student in several classes (including economics and geometry), and loved algebra.

Regarding American football, the language was foreign to me and I had to learn the plays. Thankfully, I vibed with several players on the football team because of their effort and fearless spirit. Our running back and linebacker was Doss. Kayla, another running back and defensive back, rotated with Doss a lot. Kayla was a good example of the phrase "It's not the size of the dog in the fight, but the size of the fight in the dog." Kayla was rather small, but very quick and football smart. Doss could knock anyone out on any given day in practice or in a game. We had two very gifted defensive ends, Reggie and Rakeem. I'm sure the quarterbacks and running backs of the opposing teams were not very fond of those two. They were sack masters. Playing football with my teammates was another getaway from the furnace of life. The McGavock Raiders finished with an 8-3 football record my first year playing football. I eventually became a starter on the team as a defensive end and ran track too in high school. I was also a member of a fraternity in high school called Omega Phi Gamma. I met many cool friends. Despite all the parties we attended and all the girls that liked me, I remained the "good guy."

During my junior and senior years in high school, my mom, sister, and I attended a megachurch called Hermitage Hills Baptist church. The church must have had 99 percent members of European descent. I learned that Sunday is the most segregated day in the United States regarding the Christian faith that teaches love, especially in the South. Before mom could afford a car, apart from school, we walked everywhere (even to church and to Kroger food store about half a mile from home). The automatic attention we got as black members of a majority white church was uncomfortable for me. I did not mind attending Sunday school; however, I disliked attending the regular worship service.

Sunday school got better after meeting my first mentor, Todd. He and his family are of European descent. He and his wife, Cindy, devoted their time to teaching high school students Bible study. He was a good friend, a University of TN football fan, and a man who truly exercised the Christian faith in his lifestyle. He was faithful to his wife and a good father to his children, Zach, Hunter, and Gracie. Mr. Todd, his two sons, and I attended football, baseball, and basketball games periodically.

Prior to graduating from McGavock High School with a faculty award (an award given to a graduating senior by the faculty), I was puzzled over a situation involving drawing and painting the high school mascot that ended badly. I was one of the best artists in high school, although I will say a fellow classmate by the name of Michael was better. I loved my fine arts class. My teacher and I agreed that I would draw the school's mascot (a raider riding on a stallion and holding a flag with a McGavock High symbol) on the first-floor main wall of the school's library entrance. Every day after school, I was busy working on the project. Classmates and teachers cheered me on. After I finished drawing in pencil, several people said, "Great job! It looks good." The next stage was painting. I had a conversation with my art teacher about mixing white and black paint. He was totally supportive. I also expressed the idea that the mixture symbolizes the school's diversity. I began painting the mascot. It looked great. However, one morning I entered the school and discovered that the entire artwork had been painted over. The deep confusion I experienced at that moment was strong. That moment was one of the many hundreds of rejection moments I experienced in the furnace of life. My art teacher was not at fault. He explained to me that some people in authority did not like the idea behind the color of the raider on the horse.

I worked at Captain D's my senior year in high school. My supervisor's name was Tim. Working at Captain D's was fun and humbling, and it gave me a new perspective on life. As a cook and server, I learned so much about the speed of the fast-food industry. My coworkers ranged from young to old and from white to Hispanic to black. A typical workday involved clocking in, and then updating promotional signs for customers to see the special for the day. Afterward, I started battering and frying fish. I also brought out the chicken strips, breadsticks, hush puppies, and french fries and started frying them too, while making sure shrimps, oysters, crabs, and flounders are stocked in a close by fridge. Captain D's also offered baked alternatives, including fish, potato, chicken, vegetables, and shrimp. I loved preparing orders because I learned to make them so quickly. Lunch was on the restaurant. Tim and I got along very well.

I helped close the restaurant sometimes. The responsibilities included cleaning, sweeping, mopping, taking the trash out, and sometimes washing the dishes. I didn't mind. However, some days were challenging when I started to think about other things. I once suggested to Tim how cool a floating Captain D's would be. He agreed. I got the idea after visiting St. Louis and eating at the floating McDonald's close to the famous St. Louis arch. It just made sense to have a floating

Captain D's: a seafood restaurant. Upper-level managers often came to the Captain D's where I worked to eat and for meetings. The team made sure they left impressed. Our customers were treated very well.

I hope the first four chapters have communicated that progress is a steady path. Sometimes it doesn't come quickly. With a positive attitude, good work ethic, and humility, anyone can overcome the odds regardless of background and upbringing. The ultimate choice to not let our bad experiences dictate our future depends on us.

Chapter 5
COLLEGE LIFE,
FURNACE OF LIFE – NASHVILLE, TN

In 2001, MOM and I had a conversation about whether I should attend a training school to become a pilot or go to a four-year university and major in aeronautical and Industrial technology. In addition to my fascination with airplanes, I had a strong interest in building construction and engineering. Although numerous schools accepted me, I chose to stay in Nashville, Tennessee and attended Tennessee State University (TSU). In-school tuition was less expensive, and I used a combination of scholarship, grants, and loans to pay for school, books, and housing. In addition, two of my close high school friends, Jerome and Mike, attended TSU. It seemed like yesterday that Jerome, Mike, and I enrolled, were admitted, and resided at Watson Residence Hall at TSU. We stayed in a triple room our freshman year. It is proper to say a few things about my two close high school friends.

Jerome was a ladies' man, clean cut, and musically gifted. He played the saxophone very well, very energetic, and we both liked talking about geometrical shapes, roman numerals, and masonic and Greek symbols. Mike was a starter on the football team, liked rap music, and liked to imitate a wrestler, "The Rock" Dwayne Johnson (who is also an actor well known in the Fast and Furious movie series). We were all popular, funny, and excelled academically. It was rare to not see us three together those days.

Freshman-year college life was fun. A typical week started with all three of us eating breakfast together, before morning classes. After morning classes, we ate lunch together. At times, we walked the campus and reminisced on high school days. We also had conversations about women. Mike and Jerome had girlfriends. I did not (by choice). We joked a lot about their relationships. They liked to point out women to me and encouraged me to approach them. My various replies: "I am not going to stick my thing in anything." "You see this bottle? I prefer a full one, instead of half full." "I am focused." "Physical attraction is not love." These replies were funny, genuine, and personal.

The experience of my parents' problems influenced me to not rush into a relationship with a woman. I sometimes wished I were in a relationship, wanted to give the women I liked and who liked me a chance, and thought about sex every now and then. However, I was too focused. Trust me, I liked women and enjoyed their company. At the same time, it was very hard for a woman to distract me. I still appreciated and encouraged women anyway. I treated all the women I met in high school and college like sisters, nothing more. By the way, I am not attracted to men. I struggled with tolerating gays and lesbians. The idea of men liking men and women liking women was not natural to me. However, I eventually learned it is important to treat all humans (gay, straight, or lesbian) equally with respect, liberty, and rights provided by the law of the land. Despite if I did not personally support the same-sex lifestyle, I understood that gays and lesbians too have a story and deserve respect in professional and social settings.

College life gave Jerome, Mike, and I the opportunity to meet new friends like Theo. We met him in the same residence hall. Theo liked music, sports, highly intelligent in math, physics, programing, and was a respected upperclassman. We met at the main cafeteria for dinner. After dinner and taking care of class work and exercising, we all met in our room to talk, play Madden or Mortal Combat, or watch a movie. Theo's advice led me to my first college scholarship during a conversation about alternative ways to pay for school. He suggested that I apply for a National Science Foundation scholarship and informed me about the requirements. I did, got the scholarship, and it helped me for several semesters with college expenses and limited the amount of loans I took.

In the residence hall, the fire alarm got pulled sometimes and community restrooms were vandalized by unknown childish residents. We disliked this, especially when the alarm got pulled after midnight. It disrupted the sleep of the students that came to college for the right reasons and forced us to pay a community fine.

Jerome and I attended his mother's church for a while. Mike attended church with his mom. I eventually attended Mt. Zion Baptist Church, a megachurch that most of the college students within Nashville and the surrounding areas attended. Mt. Zion, by the way, provided round-trip transportation and food. Bishop Joseph Walker delivered a relatable word to the church. By the way, one of Bishop Walker's messages reminded me that all my life struggles, barriers, and adversity only made me stronger. The truth is they did. I am thankful that God blessed me with a spirit to persevere. I am very resourceful and persistent, with a humble confidence, and very calm (even in the worst of situations). At the age of 29, I still do not have a girlfriend or potential wife. I am working on it. I am fishing and hope to recognize the right fish: my true companion, my helper, my friend, my wife, and the one I believe God ordained for me. The one I will love, hold, encourage, be faithful to, serve with, and lead with.

By the end of my first year in college, I decided to change my major from aeronautical and industrial technology to architectural and facilities engineering because of my love for building, engineering, and construction. Jerome, Mike, and I wanted to go through the Omega Psi Phi Fraternity membership process around this time. We were in a related Greek letter fraternity in high school. However, the Rho Psi chapter was inactive for years on TSU 's college campus. It was interesting that I eventually became a member of Alpha Phi Alpha Fraternity years later after researching Greek letter organizations. I made the right decision. Dr. Martin Luther King Jr is an Alpha man. Jerome transferred to Western Kentucky around our sophomore year. Mike eventually transferred to Austin Peay University.

As a second-year college student and first-year engineering major, I felt the furnace of life start to become hotter. I felt like an outsider among other engineering students who were more familiar with the engineering environment, faculties, and the dean. I knew the engineering program would take at least five years to complete. Something in me decided to hold on, stay strong, and press on. Music, reading the Bible, exercising, and the opportunity to become one of the fullbacks for the TSU football team were my temporary escapes from the furnace of life. The flame got hotter and wider, with continuous internship rejections fueling the flame.

By the beginning of my third year in college and my second year as an engineering major, I became so strong physically, got faster, and decided to play college football. In addition to football, I was very involved as a leader on TSU's Campus. One of my teammates, Troy Smith, invited some football players to Tiger Victory Fellowship (which was later renamed to Every Nation Campus Ministries - ENCM). Balancing football practice with engineering was not easy. After practice in the evening, I had to study for tests, quizzes, or work on engineering projects. I stayed up until 2, 3, or 4 a.m. at times. Sometimes I didn't get any sleep and had to be ready for an 8 a.m. class. I couldn't afford to fail any class. The college loans and interest I had to pay increased. I had no time for social activities.

I eventually became a starting fullback and my understanding of American football was much better. After a football game, a team victory, and blocking well for the running backs, it came to a shock when I found out I was not invited to camp for the next season. My team mates were shocked as well. I discovered that the coaches were divided about the decision. It seemed my academic pursuits were an obstacle; one coach advised me to consider choosing to be an undecided major so I could continue playing football. I was looking forward to a football scholarship to help mitigate my student loans. I was getting less grants and the National Science Foundation Scholarship that supported my education had a time limit. I had to make a tough decision after being advised by that coach to change my major to undecided and play football. I decided to remain an engineering major and walked away from the game I loved.

Moving forward, I had to find a reliable alternative to make some money and to start paying off my student loan and interest as an undergraduate. Around that time, I was a elected president of the residence hall council and appointed president of Every Nation Campus Ministries at Tennessee State University. During the summer time, I also chose to be a pre-college program counselor at the College of Engineering, Technology, and Computer Science. I mentored and taught high school students different types of subjects, including math and algebra, introduced them to engineering principles, and helped them develop their presentation skills.

It was also during this period that I got to know the dean of the College of Engineering, Technology, and Computer Science. Many students, including myself, had difficulty communicating with him. He seemed arrogant and unapproachable, particularly due to his tendency to walk away in the middle of conversations. It gave the impression that he did not care. Eventually I realized his behavior was due to his standards. He expected students to possess a high level of maturity and professionalism, to present themselves well, and to demonstrate knowledge. Those students who did not meet these standards had a hard time getting through to him. Dr. Decatur Rogers is his name.

Success in the professional world is harder for African Americans (especially black men) to attain. It is like we must be two to three times better than the average Caucasian or white male to be respected and allowed to earn the same opportunity. Dr. Rogers understood this and was strategically preparing all the students for this reality. We must fight to be successful, suffer for it, and persevere towards it despite the obstacles. The real world, if we were ill prepared, would take us, eat us alive, and spit out the remains. We had to be mentally prepared to deal with that reality of racism and prejudice in corporate and social American environment. As a black man himself, Dr. Rogers understood that and he did a great job of preparing all students that had the luxury of having him as a teacher. It was an honor that I took and passed Dr. Rogers' thermodynamics class, after three attempts. Thermodynamics was the only class I took three times. Thermodynamics, with Dr. Rogers as a teacher, was much more than reading, studying, retaining, and knowing the material or passing all tests, quizzes, and submitting homework in time. Very few engineering students passed this class on the first attempt; most passed after a second or third attempt; and some took four to six attempts before passing. Some never did. Why? Dr. Rogers went beyond theory in the classroom. He made sure to prepare his students for life after college.

A typical class included Dr. Rogers walking in with such an authority that commanded immediate silence. Only a few students dared to sit in the first two rows of the classroom. Most sat at the back. After walking in, he normally put his book, folders, and documents on the table. He took out a marker, approached the board slowly, and wrote down the definition of thermodynamics: the science of energy and entropy and the study of properties and substances that have a relationship to energy and entropy. Afterward, he began to lecture on the next chapter in the textbook to prepare students for the next homework. He sometimes asked, in one of his famous phrases, "If we can get someone to go to the board. . . ." while laughing. This phrase was a signal for whoever dared to, whoever was prepared enough, and whoever was strong minded to step up and lead the class in a homework assignment. The timid students sat down and remained quiet. Other popular phrases of Dr. Rogers, as my classmates should still be familiar with, were "Let's not make it mystical (while laughing)" or "Thermo system. . . physical system. . . open system. . . steady state, steady flow."

Dr. Rogers was the best teacher I had ever had. Thermodynamics class was both challenging and fun. He had a very low tolerance for mistakes, regardless if it was a quiz, a test, an exam, or the order of solving engineering problems. In fact, he preferred no mistakes. Students constantly took both word and problem quizzes. They prepared us for tests. If we answered or defined a word correctly but left out a period or comma, it was wrong. He even graded using a negative. I am laughing right now as I write. If the answer to a engineering test, exam, or quiz was right, but any part of the process he taught to show how the solution was reached was missing, he gave a negative.

By the way, students had to make up those negative scores to pass the class. The negative scores had the potential to turn an A student to a C student and a B student to a D or F student at the end of the semester after total scores from exams, tests, and quizzes were added. We were the best of the best, period (either at TSU or at any college in America). As his students, we just had a presence about us that warranted respect on campus. I am grateful I had Dr. Rogers as a teacher. It was because of him that his thermodynamics students who graduated have engineering jobs, are leaders in their field, owners-partners in many fields, or are leaders in the community. He was very big on community service too. A teacher like Dr. Decatur Rogers is rare. He made sure students earned the engineering scholarships and assistance he offered. He prepared us for life, showed us how to deal with failure, and guided us on how to approach problems or obstacles. He thought me some key important lessons about life my dad never did. Some of those lessons I learned from Dr. Rogers are the importance of preparation, community involvement, embracing failure, courage to try again and again, humility, leadership, helping a fellow human being, and the benefits of laughter and being calm in the most stressful and challenging situations.

After two summers of working as a pre-college program counselor, I decided to become a resident assistant (RA) in Hale Residence Hall. I had no clue that this decision would lead all the way to almost six years as a Department of Residence Life staff member (with about three years as a full-time director at the age of twenty-three). I was an RA for two years, first in Hale Residence Hall and then Henry A. Boyd Residence Hall. My first two years in residence life gave me the opportunity to serve fellow college students. I helped with room maintenance, check-in, check-out, and repair requests. I tutored in several subjects, conducted career and leadership forums or events, and mentored many. However, my personality covered up the fact that I was dealing with rejection after rejection in my aim to attain an engineering internship or co-op. A co-op is like a job a student takes in his or her field and often requires leaving school for a few semesters to get on the job experience. The student eventually resumes school after the job experience.

Eventually, I had an engineering co-op offer that required me to put school on pause for a few semesters, move to another state, and pay initial expenses. I was very concerned about putting my engineering education on pause, moving out of Tennessee, and not being able to afford the initial costs of moving and living on my own. I did not even have a car. At the time, the thought of moving to any other state where I did not know anyone was a concern. If I knew what I know now back then, I would have taken that co-op in a heartbeat because I finally realized the importance of stepping out of my comfort zone. I could have considered other avenues to raise money for the initial cost of the co-op. Also, I should have known that I did not have to have a car to move around in some states. There are other forms of transportation like trains and city buses. The mistake I made was being hasty in my response to the recruiter regarding those concerns. The company did not provide initial cost of travel nor offered any assistance with living expenses upfront. I also knew my mom, although had my best interest in mind and would have helped financially if she could, was not able to.

The more I matured, the more I wished I had taken that co-op. It took me a few more semesters to get an internship. The lesson I learned later was experience in the engineering field is as important and, in some cases, more important than theory. If I had taken the co-op, I would have gained valuable on the job experience very early as a student. Experience would have provided both practical education and on-the-job training. Afterward, the more I persisted to get another internship or co-op, the more I received letters saying I had not been selected. I went to several career fairs, listened and acted on many suggestions to improve my resume, spoke to several recruiters, dressed to impress, spoke eloquently at several interviews, was sincere in my answers, and took constructive criticisms well. Despite all that, I still could not get an internship or co-op. During and after my education, all my attempts at getting a co-op, internship, or job in the engineering field resulted in over 600 rejections, one co-op offer, and one internship offer. I eventually stopped counting my rejections.

I had the GPA, the intelligence, the work ethic, and eventually the willingness to move out of state, but that was not enough I guess. At times, I wondered if my color, my accent, or the fact that I was not a U.S. citizen until 2007 had something to do with it. I was a permanent U.S. resident and in the process of becoming a U.S. citizen. All that did not matter, even after I became a U.S. citizen. They say men should not cry. I did not publicly. I understood—and want to remind my readers—those rejections and failures were part of life and led to my successes. I suffered rejections too much for so long when it came to getting a job in my field. My unending rejections forced the tears out of my eyes every now and then, alone. Despite the stress, agony, pain, frustrations, and isolation, I had to be strong for my mom, sister, mentees, students, and residents of the facilities at TSU. People (young men and women) looked up to me in and outside of Tennessee State University's campus. I had to be strong! Since I was unable to get an engineering job after earning a degree in 2007, I kept on applying for jobs in an engineering or related field. I had to take a graduate assistant job for a year in Henry A. Boyd Residence Hall and eventually stepped up as the Director of Henry A. Boyd Residence Hall for almost three years. I helped at other residence life facilities off and on TSU's campus. In addition to the management of the building(s) and residents, the job was an opportunity to help engender a positive mindset in as many young men and women as possible. Throughout those six years as a residence life staff member, I used most of the money I made to pay my student loans. I started to do this as a resident assistant, continued it as a director, and finished up paying my loans by the time I earned my MPA degree. I am thankful for the ability to do so, despite that life got harder most times in other areas. Why? Well, chapter 7: my rejections.

Chapter 6
EXERCISING AND WRITING,
FURNACE OF LIFE – NASHVILLE, TN

WORDS COULD NOT describe the level of hate for God I had by the end of 2007. Throughout the years in high school and college, despite the obstacles, I was super strong in my Christian faith. I was faithful to God, church, and family. I was very respectful and encouraged both men and women. I was diligent academically and constantly served the community. After years of prayers to God to bless me by the time I graduated with an ideal job and an ideal girlfriend-future wife, I left graduation smiling on the outside but was unhappy and hurting inside due to unanswered prayers. Allow me to say here that I desired a perfect (flawless) woman at the time because I thought I was perfect due to the way I lived my life. If I did everything right, my thought was God will bless me. I never gave the women interested in me a chance due to my mindset and my experience in early stages of my life. I was very wrong and will elaborate later why there is no such thing as a flawless or perfect woman (or human being).

The job part hurt much more because I did everything I could and acted on a lot of suggestions and advice. On the way to a graduation celebration, my Honda Accord broke down due to a transmission failure. Reality forced me to remain at Tennessee State University and to take a plan B full-time job I mentioned in chapter five. I became a director, managing residence facilities on TSU's campus. My primary facility was Boyd Hall. I helped in other residence facilities and off campus apartments. I had to keep some income flowing. On the same cold night in 2007, after I said thank you to all that attended the celebration that my mom planed for me for earning the degree, I left as an engineering graduate without a job in that field. I still wondered how I stayed calm in that critical moment. Let's just say my name is Abayomi. It means "enemies would have ridiculed me but God prevailed over them." It also means "bringer of happiness or joyful to meet." Really? Then why is it that I had to experience so much pain for being so young for so long? Yes, I brought joy to many lives. Why is it that the key things I desired were absent from mine?

Jim Laffoon, a prophet of Bethel World Outreach in Brentwood, Tennessee, prophesied regarding my future once. Bethel is a part of Every Nation Ministries led by Rice Brooks. Bethel currently has churches and campus ministries in more than seventy nations. Jim once told me I would pastor a church one day. The diversity of the Bethel church was a big attraction for me.

A unique group of college young brothers in Christ helped at Bethel World Outreach college service programs in downtown Nashville for many years with our time, talents, and treasures. We just liked to serve the church. I am also trying to make a point on how much we were in love with God and what we were willing to do to serve people. Volunteering included cleaning toilets, urinals, and general building areas prior to and after the college programs. We served as security guards, drove church vans, and put up many tables and chairs. We were college students and Christians doing whatever we could to help the church and live a life guided by the word of God. The brothers I remember are Dwayne, David, Reggie, Troy, Jonathan, Eric, Terrance, Bryan, Justin, Tyrone, Derrick, Oba, and Jazz. We were like brothers on the TSU college campus too.

Dwayne and I are like blood brothers. We have both matured together from college students to men. I have watched him go through a lot in life and overcome so much. He is now happily married to his wife, with a son and a good job too. I am so glad he never gave up because he was overlooked often and had setbacks. I am glad he persevered. From working with Dwayne when I was director of Boyd Hall, I learned he has a very good work ethic. He is a gentle, funny, athletic, intelligent, and a strong black man. We just clicked and were both on the TSU football team. Troy is a friend also. He was the one who invited Dwayne and I to Tiger Victory Fellowship after a football practice one night. Troy also played TSU football. He is very funny and a natural salesman. He likes to rap, a natural happy person, and one of the funniest people you can ever meet. He is also happily married to his wife and they have a son.

We liked to joke around too. We often joked about how Pastor Shino would say "Chaaaaaamp! What's going on—are you strong?" Pastor Shino played in the NFL, despite his small stature. He is very cool, dark skin, and one of the many pastors of Bethel. We met at the on-campus worship service Troy invited Dwayne and me to. Those words were pastor Shino's way of genuinely asking the brothers if we were struggling in our faith, in college, or with anything like identity, sin, or pride.

Our sisters helped the church too with their talents, including singing. A unique group of college sisters who also attended Bethel consisted of Tammy, LaTasha, Autumn, Tywana, Angela, Shanae, Stephanie, and Shalyn. They also loved God and liked attending Bethel. We all treated each other as brothers and sisters, with no ulterior motives. Our College campus ministers at the time were Pastor Shino, Pastor Steve, Pastor Taylor, James, Sjhira, Kami, and Jacinta.

Thinking back to how I felt when Prophet Jim Laffon prophesied I would pastor a church in the future, I need God to keep it real with me, communicate with me directly, guide me, empower me, show me his glory, and anoint me with the necessary tools to battle and win in the spirit realm on behalf of the oppressed and his kingdom. I just don't want to mislead people. Neither words nor any amount of preaching are enough these days. People need real solutions to their problems. I have seen many go through so much hurt and pain, and I helped in any way I could. I am not going to add to the pain. They deserved truth, something tangible, real solutions, and not just words. I am not going to mislead them or preach the good news when my experience with God has been mostly painful. Sometimes, it was like God was not listening and I was the only one communicating. There were too many situations where I needed God to act at that very moment, but was left hanging. Why should I preach about a God that does not care? I needed the right tools, God! All or nothing, because I knew that Satan, demons, witches, wizards, evil men, and evil women do not play fair. I just prefer to not fake it. I will rather keep it real and avoid deception.

I still remember my prophecy by Jim Laffoon of Bethel World Outreach Center in Brentwood. I was told I was a fine man and highly responsible at a young age. He said I was a man after God's own heart. I was informed that God had been molding and shaping me. It had not been an easy molding time. I was told that there were many times that I felt tired, pulled in many directions, tired, and empty. I was told that God saw me as his son. Prophet Laffoon talked about how I was always willing to give to people. Prophet Laffoon said God was going to help me and that God was going to pour out his spirit and fire on me. I was told I would have influence in the business world and in the church, that I would have an ability to make money and get money, that I was a leader of multiple nations, and that I had been yoked with Jesus Christ. His power and spirit was mine. I also remember Prophet Laffoon saying people would trust and open up to me and I have something about me that is magnetic. I remember that day very well: my silence and how accurate the prophecy was about my pain (in the furnace of life). Although I ended up breaking the CD the prophecy was recorded on years later due to more obstacles, something wouldn't allow me to forget the prophecy. I will say I am not in haste to become a pastor or lead a church. For me to do this, I need God to directly communicate to me and equip me. Too much is at stake for me to depend just on a prophet or pastor's word regarding my future. I would rather hear directly from God. Nothing else will do or convince me.

Whenever my *why* questions for God come to mind, I recall echoes of great leaders counseling my spirit. They are men of faith: Dr. Martin Luther King Jr., President Nelson Mandela, President George Washington, President Barack Obama, Maximus the Gladiator, and biblical icons: Abraham, Joseph, Job, Daniel, David, Moses, Jabez, Gideon, Jeremiah, Paul, Peter, and, most importantly, Jesus. It is like I hear their echoes saying, "Do not yield to a cheap thrill or what comes easy. Persevere." Integrity shields from temptation, lays a foundation on solid ground, and allows a man to use his talents for the greater good. My ambition to be just like them is no coincidence; it is Providence. I wanted to give up on God, but something just would not allow it.

Eric Thomas, a professional speaker, is known for saying, "When you get to the point that you want to be successful as bad as you need air, then you will be successful." I needed to be successful for people looking up to me, for my mom and sister, and for my future family. To do this, I had to stay alive!

The Apostle Paul said, "Rejoice in your suffering, for suffering produces perseverance, perseverance produces character, and character produces hope, and hope does not disappoint, because God's love has been poured into our hearts through the holy spirit."

To stay alive and sane, I continued to write and exercise. On the night I graduated with my engineering degree, the temperature was very low. It was freezing outside. It was dangerous to exercise in that temperature. I just could not tolerate my circumstance a minute longer and I chose to exercise. The obstacles (heat or furnace) of life were too much; I had to cool off, I guess. A few minutes longer doing nothing in that critical moment may have caused a serious health condition. After stretching in my room, I went outside in my blue gym shorts and blue short-sleeved shirt to run around the TSU Hale Stadium (campus football field) and then to run the stairs. Exercising on that very cold and dark night was dangerous in the clothes I had on. The furnace of life was too much to tolerate. Exercising was and still is my getaway when feeling overwhelmed. It keeps me calm. Without it, I would have gone crazy many times. I remember going back to my room, lying on the ground very tired, very weak, and being on the brink of passing out. Luckily, I didn't.

Exercising, music, and writing are like medication and a way to take my mind off stress. I honestly don't know if I would have endured the furnace without exercising. I also like to write. The following are some of my poems and thoughts:

In Planet Earth

Clear to me is one thing in planet Earth.
Love, if it will last, depends on choices made in my heart.
I might be a companion of myself for a while.
Because of neither insecurity nor lack of approachability.
Don't sell your birth right for a cheap thrill, my heart reminds.
Wait; with patience, she will eventually be found.
Stayed away from all the clubbing and everything alike.
But without a companion this heart remains.
Ignorance will say women he desires not.
But wisdom will pause and ask
Could it be his life growing up and what his eyes witnessed a lot?
Is that why his heart is seared to desire not just any woman?
Clear to me is one thing in planet Earth.
Love and physical attraction are not the same.
With attraction alone leaves infidelity an open door.
But patience comes before true love abides.
In planet Earth, I made this choice in my heart.

Faithful

Faithful to you before I knew you.

Faithful to you I long to pour my heart to.
Faithful to you I have always loved.
Faithful to my true companion, my helper, my true best friend.
Wherever you are on planet Earth,
Know that I have always been faithful.
In times of temptation, accusation, and deception,
Know that I will strive to honor the instructions of wisdom.
Faithfulness to stay away from the immoral woman.
Faithfulness to not desire another man's wife.
Faithful to be my brother's and sister's keeper.
Faithfulness to know, hold, honor, protect, and love you.
Faithfulness to have you beside me to serve, lead, and love.
Yes, I have prayed many times for you.
For your comfort, joy, peace, and protection.
Yes, I have prayed many times for you.
For my faithfulness to bless me you.
My helper, my queen, my true companion, my future wife.

And then we wonder why?

Everything created in this world was created for good. They become bad when we abuse them and then we wonder why? Men, why is it so difficult for some of us to control what is between our legs? What takes some men to that point to rape, beat, cheat, or at times kill a woman? Why has Tupac Shakur's warning of raising a generation that will hate the ladies that make the babies come true? A real man is much more than a male. A real man should cultivate a woman to become the ideal wife he desires. There is no such thing as a flawless or perfect woman as I have finally learned. A real man should protect, provide, lead, and uplift his woman (wife). A real man should strive to make things better in his community, state, and nation, using his skills, talents, and treasures. A real man should have a stable and honest job. A real man is a true father: loyal, and present for both his wife and children.

What about our environment? We live in a society, at times,

misled by its entertainment industries, news stations, churches, and government all for the sake of ratings, views, numbers, or greed. We live in a society that is greedy for gain and brainwashed to think the more money it makes, the happier it will be. On another note, some of you will kill another. This is the result of hate planted at home by some parents, environments, or cliques-gangs-crews (your people). This is the result of misguided perception (out of fear) instilled about those other folks who do not look like you, without getting the facts or getting to know his or her character. It is important to understand a man. Have you forgotten that the same color of blood runs through all hearts and keeps all alive, despite the color of the skin? We live in a society of Crips versus Bloods, Hell's Angel's versus Bandidos, Muslims versus Christians, and white versus black. What led to this childish and senseless hate? Is it a need for the survival of a race that heavily ignores the fact that all are humans first and the hue of the skin is just proof that the creator is not boring? Why have we created a society of some misguided males or gangsters, with insecure mind frames, who are victims of their own environment? Why have we created hateful, crooked, and evil cops responsible for the death of many innocent lives?

What about loyalty in marriage? It is sad that some of us have forgotten the power behind sex, which unites two spirits. We have abused our ability to produce life and traded it for fun, money, and entertainment. Are we still willing to ignore the fact that there is a difference between physical attraction and love? What happened to loyalty and those sacred oaths of marriage: in sickness and in health or in the good, bad, and ugly times? We invented condoms, but we ignore the fact that, if abused, sex or infidelity can lead to varieties of evil like divorce, hatred, lack of self-control, and, at times, abandoned children and even AIDS and other sexually transmitted diseases.

Women, some of you are slowly dying. Yet, the harassment, degrading, name calling, and drama continue. You look alive, yet you are dying inside. Some of you are misguided by what you see on TV, music videos, social media, radio stations, your childhood experiences, and maybe your financial circumstances. They got some of you thinking a big butt and a cute face is all it takes to find and keep a real man or a husband. Have you forgotten that real men and real love goes beyond the physical? Sex is important. Yes, a real man must be able to satisfy you. However, it takes more than sex to keep a man. It requires a real woman: marriage material, fitting as a wife at home, a life partner, a mother of his children, healthy (mind, body, and spirit), visionary (goal oriented), nurturer, and a woman of noble character (as described in Proverbs 23). Women, heavy drinking or too much clubbing can never resolve the pain you feel inside. The system also has turned some of you into prostitutes, strippers, and degraders of your own body for the sake of money or maybe attention.

It is not my place to judge. I understand and empathize. I believe some of you would have chosen a different path if you had the help or opportunities you desperately needed at one point. Have you forgotten that you have the final authority to bring out life? Even Tupac Shakur said, "And since a man can't make one, he has no right to tell a woman when and where to create one." Women, you are valuable. Your beauty is a blessing; stop abusing it. It helps to keep your legs closed (until he has earned it, wants to marry you, and you know he will provide, protect, and love you, and you desire to do the same). It helps to control your emotion. I know you like words, but action counts much more. It helps to look beautiful, but without degrading your body. Don't you know that you are also your brother's keeper? Be part of the change that will stop the cycle of violence against you and your children.

My brothers and my sisters, we need to consider the words of Knine (Christian rapper) who said, "Everything you say and do affects somebody else not just you, so why don't you take a minute or two and think before you make a move."

I have seen a lot, including the physical and mental abuse I saw between my parents. I have also witnessed and stopped domestic violence against women, broken up fights started for senseless reasons between males and between females, and experienced racism and prejudice in its many modern forms.

I wrote so much in college. Writing, regardless if it is for school or at work, just became second nature. Allow me to end this chapter with a basic guiding principle:

> *Blessed is the man who does not walk in the counsel of the wicked or stand in the way of sinners or sit in the seat of mockers. But his delight is in the law of the LORD, and on his law, he meditates day and night. He is like a tree planted by streams of water, which yields its fruit in season and whose leaf does not wither. Whatever he does prospers. Not so the wicked! They are like chaff that the wind blows away. Therefore, the wicked will not stand in the day judgment, nor sinners in the assembly of the righteous. For the LORD watches over the way of the righteous, but the way of the wicked will perish. (Psalms.1.1-6, NIV version)*

Chapter 7
TRAINING GROUND,
FURNACE OF LIFE – NASHVILLE, TN

For almost three years, I managed Henry Allen Boyd Residence Hall, a seven-floor residential facility with 372 spaces as a director. Henry Allen Boyd is a founder of Tennessee State University, by the way, which makes it a historic building. I constantly helped in other facilities and on campus apartments too. I often wished I managed a more appealing facility that required all students to have at least a 3.0 GPA or higher. This was not the case. I dealt with guns, gangs, thieves, noises, vandalism, saggin (wearing short or long pants-jeans below the waist), smoking, fire, and constantly clogged toilets, drains, and urinals. Most residents were focused and good students. Some of the focused ones eventually became leaders on and off campus. They were elected to positions like Mr. Tennessee State University, Representative at Large, student government association presidents and vice presidents, and presidents of other respective organizations at the university. Many even became resident assistants or work-study students at the facility I managed, in other residence halls, and on campus apartments. Several of these young men (and women) that I mentored currently still communicate with me. The resident assistants I supervised had to be strong-minded to work in Boyd Hall. We did our best to report maintenance and repair requests to facilities management as quickly as possible. The resident assistants were like my brothers. I showed no favoritism as a director and set high standards for them academically.

The facility management employees that serviced the residence halls and apartments were as prompt and polite as they could be, despite their limited resources. Unfortunately, Henry A. Boyd Hall had a lot of cover-up repairs and maintenance work done in previous years, but the staff that cleaned the building was as humble and calm as could be. The cleaning alone made the building tolerant to reside in, but the building just needed a major renovation. Some residents couldn't wait to get out and reside in other more appealing residential facilities. I did the same thing as an undergraduate student. For almost three years, I was persistent with sending email after email to my supervisors and top-level administrators. The emails informed them about the need to replace constantly stuck elevators, to correct plumbing issues leading to constantly clogged toilets, to replace peeling insulation on HVAC pipes in most rooms, and to remove vulgar graffiti on the building's exterior wall. I suggested renovation ideas and recommended many disciplinary sanctions for those that violated residence life policies and procedures. I like to credit Modena, the previous director who trained me and believed in me, for my ability to be a director. Before he transitioned to a better opportunity at another university, he trained me so well as a resident assistant, his assistant director, and advocated on my behalf to the dean of residence life at the time that I was very qualified and ready to become a director (despite being so young).

The Department of Residence Life did help with minor and urgent facility needs. Henry A. Boyd Hall had many facility issues mentioned above, due to the age of the building. I persisted for about three years with emails and informed officials within the departments of residence life and student affairs about the need to act on these repairs. The assistant director of residence life once told me that funds were limited and the department had other important priorities. I did not like that it was taking so long to make needed repairs. I was still getting letters of rejection from the engineering companies I wanted to work for. I was stressed and felt drained.

I felt betrayed and not appreciated by God, whom I earnestly strived to honor with my lifestyle. I eventually started to struggle spiritually, but never allowed the furnace of life to lead me to destruction, drinking, fighting, quitting, or any other negative things that circumstances can engender. For some reason, I remained focused. I believed that one day, better days would come.

The building I managed needed an assistant director, in addition to the resident assistants I had. I barely had time for myself. Even after office hours, I was still on the job. As a residence hall director (in my very early twenties), I had to stay in the building. I had to help residents who needed it. I was responsible for lives in the building. We kept many strangers from walking into the building, but a few robberies occurred. Ninety-five percent of our efforts to make the building safe prevailed, but that five percent of problems misrepresented Henry A. Boyd Hall at times.

It reached the point that I started to put myself in harm's way to confront locals (nonstudents) and break up fights between students and residents. I constantly informed my supervisors in writing and verbally as respectfully and professionally as I could regarding the need to implement the safety suggestions I proposed. I risked losing my job, but that did not matter. In my mind, the residents and students deserved better for what they paid to reside in the building. I even encouraged residents (student leaders) to join me and demand better living conditions. In the beginning of my last two semesters as the director, the heat, ventilation, and air conditioning pipes' insulation were replaced in the rooms that needed the repairs. I was also informed of future plans to replace the elevators. The vulgar graffiti was finally removed. The community showers were fitted with new drain covers and plumbing work was done in the building. Finally, Henry A. Boyd Hall got some attention regarding maintenance and repair. It helped.

At the same time, the residence hall had another issue with crowd control. The location of the building was not remote like other residential facilities. Therefore, it was easy access for the locals. For some reason, students and residents of other residential facilities liked to gather in front of the hall as locals would. By the time I stepped up to manage the facility, I was also in graduate school working towards a master's in public administration. I still had no assistant director at the time. The resident assistants, security, and I did all we could to ensure the safety of the students and residents. However, TSU security often advised me that we couldn't make the crowd leave. They had the right to assemble if they weren't blocking the driveway. The fact was they did sometimes. This was frustrating! I was tired and drained due to countless moments I had to come out of the director's apartment to tell several residents and locals to turn down loud music, not smoke in front of the building, and not yell in front of the building because residents were complaining. I had to be the support for my resident assistants, who were students themselves, to confront the few bad residents who were throwing objects out of the window, pulling fire alarms, saggin, smoking, and gambling in the building. The fact is, some of my recommendations for disciplinary action did not get supported. This made the job harder not only on me but also on the resident assistants.

Managing the residence hall was like managing a city. We had responsible, outgoing, intelligent, and very involved students and leaders. We also had the gangsters and troublemakers. I endured sleepless nights, tired days, stressful mornings, and lonely hours. I felt trapped at times. I barely left campus, unless I had to go get groceries, visit mom occasionally, or go to my graduate classes after 4:30 p.m. I also left campus after school semester ended to help drive the Department of Residence Life van full of clothes and items donated by students and residents of all TSU residential facilities. The items were donated to the rescue mission annually. When I came back from graduate classes around 8 pm, I still worked to ensure the safety of all residents. I was unhappy due to my continued rejections from attempts to get a job in an engineering field, but I was the leader and I just could not quit, especially in the middle of a semester. I had to set positive examples for students and resident assistants who were striving to better themselves and be successful. For them, I finished the semester. I remained calm and did not allow adversity to break me down. An assistant director was hired eventually, and he left after just one semester.

After almost three years, my last semester as a full-time residence life staff made me felt both uncertain and happy about the future. Yes, I had some good memories. I am still thankful that I had the opportunity to help bring additional improvements to the facility and positively influence students. I told my supervisor that I would be resigning by choice. I did.

After visiting Boyd Hall and TSU a few years later when my life circumstances had improved, with a new job as a Grants Manager for the Tennessee Department of Labor and Workforce Development, I was very pleased to see a gate surrounding Boyd Hall. The lesson I wish to teach or remind the reader here is persistence can move mountains. It helps to keep planting the seed and to never underestimate the days of small beginnings. Eventually, things can get better with a positive attitude and calm approach.

Prior to my new job as mentioned above, my persistence to get a job in the construction or engineering field seemed almost victorious. More important, my mind, spirit, and soul just needed the change and rest from TSU and residence life. I spoke to an owner-CEO of a construction company who informed me that I would be called for a job after the end of my last semester as director of Boyd Hall. Even if I didn't call, I was told I would be contacted. This news influenced me to meet with my staff. I informed them of my plans to move on after the end of spring 2011 semester. I also graduated with a master's in public administration in 2011. I wanted to visit Nigeria around that time too, but circumstances did not allow it. I did resign.

The mistake I made was I didn't make sure I got the job before resigning from the Department of Residence Life. Big mistake! But, is it right to blame me when my spiritual, mental, and physical health were slowly fading? Is it just to remain trapped in a work environment that wouldn't give me the chance to live a balanced life, seriously consider dating, or make time for the girl I liked at the time? Is it just to remain in a position that required work seven days a week, at times twenty-four hours a day, with little or no sleep most times? Although the construction company didn't call me and I didn't have a job after leaving my position in residence life, it was okay. I felt like I escaped what could have further drained me and affect my health negatively. At least I kept seeking better days from the furnace of life with more time devoted to job hunting, resting, and getting my mind back to normal. I felt like a failure during that period in my life, but I was still alive. I was still hopeful. I had been at the Tennessee State University (TSU) campus as a college student, graduate student, and staff member for a combined eleven straight years. I needed to see the world beyond TSU and had no regrets for choosing to move forward after eleven years. I was in my mid-twenties by that time. I have the character and spirit of an eagle. Eagles are not meant to be trapped. We exist to soar to highest of heights. I will have victory over my obstacles.

Chapter 8
HARD KNOCK LIFE,
FURNACE OF LIFE – NASHVILLE, TN

IF YOU HAVE ever watched the movie Rocky IV, before Rocky (played by Sylvester Stallone) faced the Russian boxer Drago (played by Dolph Lundgren) in the ring, Rocky and his wife, Adrian (played by Talia Shire) had a deep conversation. Adrian told Rocky he can't win. This statement was not because Adrian did not love Rocky or did not believe in him. As a woman and wife, she was just scared of losing her husband. One of Rocky's best friends and a boxer, Apollo Creed (played by Carl Weathers), was killed by Drago during a boxing match. Rocky felt obligated as a friend, a citizen of United States of America, and a warrior to confront the evil done by Drago. Rocky replied, "Oh, Adrian. Adrian always tells the truth. No maybe I can't win. Maybe the only thing I can do is just take everything he's got. But to beat me he's gonna have to kill me, and to kill me he's gotta have the guts to stand in front of me, and to do that he's gotta be willing to die himself. I don't know if he's ready to do that. I don't know. I don't know."

I had nothing to lose after the reality became clear that I wouldn't be employed at the job I thought I had. From that moment, the adversary made sure I felt those words: You can't win (you can't get a job; you are a failure). The significant lesson I desire to teach or remind readers from here forward is that we must be willing to face our fears. We must act and not depend on faith alone, even if the result realistically can be failure, death, total loss, or humiliation. After I resigned by choice from my position at TSU, I became a jobless twenty-seven-year-old with engineering and MPA degrees, living at his mother's apartment temporarily.

That period was one of the curve balls in my life. I appreciated Mom, her kind words, and that she allowed me to stay with her until I became employed. However, I saw what my mother couldn't see. I saw a deeper trap. I felt a hotter furnace. Starting as a senior in high school, I was used to financially supporting myself, working. I am also thankful that a combination of scholarship, loans, and grants (thanks to my TSU financial aid advisor) supplemented that effort when I transitioned to college. I still had to work my way through college to start paying back those loans, to provide my living expenses before I became a staff of residence life, and to buy food, clothes, and pay some of my tuition fees, transportation, etc. Mom gave advice but was unable to financially support me. Suddenly, I had to stay with her to save money on living expenses. That was a low point because life had put me where I didn't want to be as an educated black man with two advanced degrees, living with his mother at the age of twenty-seven for nine months. I am thankful though that she was helpful. However, I was not comfortable in that situation.

That does something to a man accustomed to major responsibilities, taking care of people, and taking many roles of leadership starting at a young age. It can slowly kill his spirit if he allows it. It can turn him inward. It can make him lose interest socially, causing him to isolate himself out of shame. It can make him feel like a nobody. That man was me for a moment. I started to question my ability to get any job worthy of my talents, skills, strengths, work ethic, and degrees. However, I did not allow myself to fall and stay in a trap that plays the victim expecting people to feel sorry. This is a very important point I also like to make. In life, do not allow the enemy or obstacles to cause you to isolate yourself or sit down doing nothing.

Do not sit down on your ass while hoping and waiting for a miraculous sign, intervention, or some angel from heaven to show up to rescue you and fight your battles. Ladies and gentlemen, you must get up, act, and save yourself to prevent that downward spiral or deeper hole. Trust me, it is easier said than done. I know it's hard. I can feel your pain; I've been there. I guarantee you that if you take just one step of action, then the next, and maybe a few more steps, you can redeem and save yourself no matter how impossible or hard the situation may be. It's a matter of choice and action. You may have to go through hell, pain, or endure a lot of rejections. However, don't quit. I promise you it will be worth it at the end. It brings joy and strength. Ask for help too. There is no shame in it, but make sure you're helping yourself. Wake up daily, meditate, pray even when it feels like God is not listening, encourage yourself, exercise to help fight the stress, eat something, get out there, network, hustle, grind, be on time, go get it, and don't forget to enjoy life.

After six months passed, with many applications and letters of rejection, I invested in an ASUS laptop and downloaded AutoDesk Revit 2011, a tool that architects use for residential or facility design, remodeling, and preconstruction. I spoke with a good friend, Carol, on the phone and told her the aphorism "success is when preparation meets opportunity" is something I fully believe. Therefore, I continued to read books from classes I took as an engineering major and public administration major. There were days when I wasn't driven at all because my situation was too much to bear. There were times when I kept a strong composure despite tears running down my face. There were moments that I just sat down silent for hours and days. Something, however, wouldn't let me give up. One day, my mom mentioned that someone she worked with needed an architect for plans to build a boys' quarter (family home) in Lagos, Nigeria, with six bedrooms, three kitchens, three living rooms, and three restrooms. I provided my first client, Dr. Felix, with three different blueprints for the home. The blueprints took a little over two weeks to complete. He chose the one he liked most out of the three different designs I did. I was paid for the job. That project gave me hope.

I desired success. Dr. Felix introduced me to a professional architect. Although the architect didn't hire me, he allowed me to lead a project for his client. I wasn't getting paid, but I was doing something I liked. I finished my second project for the second client who ran a day care on Jefferson Street in Nashville, TN. My second client didn't move forward with building and remodeling his existing day care due to financial constraints. However, he liked the design. I kept a good attitude despite not getting paid for the hours and sleepless nights I endured while getting the project done. The good thing is this second client told someone else about me. That is how I met another client and building remodeling contractor (Berry King) within that year. I provided him a building plan for a banquet hall based in Nashville. The Department of Building Codes and Standards required this plan from him in order to renovate the building. I got paid this time for helping him with this project. He was given a permit to renovate the building. Business slowed down. I needed more clients to keep the revenue flowing, but it didn't happen for a while. Later, I did similar work for a different daycare owner (Mrs. Antonia Obeto). She was also required by the Department of Building Codes and Standards to provide a building and sign plan for a project. This plan was also approved and she was given a permit to do the project. I got paid for this project.

Once again, business slowed down. I visited a mechanic. He happened to be looking for summer help and wanted someone who could create a business plan with him. I told him I could help, and he hired me. He loved the finished product and offered to give me a chance to help manage his automotive company in the summer. That experience challenged me. I did more salesman work than managing. Project management is one of my strengths, but the owner and his wife were already managing the company. I guess he mentioned management initially to get me interested in helping him with something else (sales) in addition to providing him with the business model mentioned earlier. I agreed to work with him.

On several occasions, I remember standing and walking on the street of Charlotte Pike in Nashville advertising the services of the automotive mechanic shop to the many cars driving by. I didn't mind. I had to do what I had to do, with no room for pride. It was one of my many humbling experiences in life though. I went to college campuses to sell the automotive company's services. I put hundreds of coupons and flyers on cars. I went to many apartments and houses in Nashville and outside the city areas (with barking and angry dogs) to distribute the automotive company's flyers on every door. I set up meetings with car dealers like Honda and many others in Nashville and the surrounding areas to convince them to partner with the automotive company. Some of my efforts as a salesman and part- time manager paid off. Some people came to get window tints, oil changes, vehicle repairs, and maintenance. However, we needed more customers and the owner desired more profits for the company.

The season I was a salesman was slow for independent automotive companies. We made no excuses. The environment at the shop got tense at times. I was making $150 to $300 every two weeks in 2012? Something was not right about that. As a former director and administrator who was on salary for managing residential facilities, my new financial situation was humbling. I needed more revenue. I had a meeting with the owner. He informed me that he was struggling with paying rent and paying all his employees. He had a wife, a son, and two other employees he was supporting. By the way, the owner was a very talented mechanic. He could work on most cars, foreign or American made. He was gifted. He implemented the business model I provided for his business and is now doing much better. I moved on afterwards. I chose to do what Rocky did. I was ready to confront more obstacles at all cost, knowing this decision had a 95% chance to destroy me from within. What did I do? Well, chapter 9 reveals a significant point in my life in which I faced fear head on and stepped up to a new dimension of manhood.

Chapter 9
A New Level of Manhood,
Furnace of Life – Nashville, TN

AFTER EXITING THE door of the automotive company, getting into my green Honda Accord, driving straight down Charlotte Pike towards downtown Nashville, I started focusing on my next move. A day before, I had planned to move into a place in the Gallatin-Madison area. I had a tough decision to make. I could keep staying with Mom, save the living expenses, and move out when I got the job I desired, or, by contrast, I could have the courage to move into my own place.

Two roads diverged in a wood, and I took the one less traveled by, and that has made all the difference. - Robert Frost

That same day, I went to several local businesses, including Wal-Mart and Home Depot, to ask if they were hiring. I was desperate for a job and had to have one to not deplete all my savings, even if it wasn't my ideal job. Laziness is not in my blood. All the companies I went to said they were not currently hiring, but one. After leaving Wal-Mart, something convinced me to check if Lowe's was hiring. It was. Despite that it was a seasonal job, I filled out the online application as soon as possible and I was called for an interview within a week. I was hired as one of the two assemblers and builders for all types of products. Reggie was the other assembler. We worked well together.

Summer 2012 was a cool time. The last summer I had experienced a ray of hope was 2007 when I had the opportunity to intern at the National Aeronautics and Space Administration (NASA). It was my practicum. I had fun building, calibrating, and programming three-wheel model vehicles—robots that would perform several commands. I even rewired the electrical components of the robots so they could use solar panels as an alternative technology. The solar panels stored energy from the sun into rechargeable batteries to provide power to the robots. It was also interesting researching space and moon habitation. I also proposed a subsystem for an enclosed habitat. NASA accepted the conceptual design of the subsystem I proposed.

At Lowe's in summer 2012, I assembled power and drive lawn mowers, charcoal and gas grills, outdoor kitchens, tillers and aerators, benches, and chairs. I love building things using blueprints and seeing them come to life; it's who I am. My place was less than four miles from my job. As a result, I often took advantage of extra naps. I was hired as a seasonal employee; however, I needed a full-time job. Before I started working at Lowe's and after moving on from my job in residence life, I remembered I went to the construction site of the new Nashville Music City Center to inquire about possible job opportunities as a manager or engineer. With follow-up that lasted up to a year, I found out a project engineer job was available. However, I was told I couldn't do the job. I kept a positive attitude anyway. I wanted that job and knew I could perform its duties. Remember, it's important to want to be successful as badly as you want to breathe.

Instead of simply filling out resumes and applications for companies I was interested in, I changed strategy and started going to these companies in person. I also asked friends and acquaintances who worked at the companies I was interested in to speak to the decision makers on my behalf to allow me the opportunity to earn a full-time job.

My strategy paid off. I remember receiving a call from the HR personnel linked with the Music City Center about an opportunity to work as a facility manager. This was also the same period that I found out that the Tennessee Department of Labor and Workforce Development (TDLWD) was interested in employing me as a full-time Grants Program Manager. I never experienced this before. I was used to rejection after rejection and had settled for jobs that required little of my talents and skills for years. This time, one of the jobs available (the state job) was related to my MPA degree. It also required some of the tools and skills I used managing Henry A. Boyd Residence Hall. I had to decide. The thought of managing another completed facility was not as close to my heart as having a career in the building construction field as a project manager, engineer, or getting the opportunity to do something with my MPA. After much thought, I chose to be a Grants Program Manager for the TDLWD. I made this decision because it gave me an opportunity to gain experience in accounting, financial management, contracts, procurement, and analyzing numbers. I enjoyed working with numbers. I helped managed a budget of around $50,000,000 annually, which helped fund thirteen local workforce investment areas in the ninety-five counties in Tennessee.

My experience at TDLWD was both rewarding and challenging. A spirit of prejudice and a struggle between different races and within the same race existed in the state government. When I was hired, both the commissioner and deputy that led TDLWD were African American women. I still remember the interview I had with Commissioner Karla Davis and Deputy Alisa Malone like it was yesterday. It was good to know that two women (who happened to be African American) were leading hundreds of other leaders from many backgrounds, races, ages, and creeds.

Deputy was a confident, down-to-earth, generous, and energetic leader. Her motor just kept going and going until the job was done. She was also a great speaker who could capture the crowd's attention and maintain an upbeat spirit in the room. Deputy cared about the success of workers at the department and insisted that they get the training and opportunity necessary to be effective and efficient at the job. Her initiative to make sure my TDLWD supervisor moved forward regarding the last statement makes her legit.

Commissioner was an intelligent woman. Point blank. She was also humble and open to suggestions. A meeting I had with her validated to me that integrity, a caring heart, clarity, and progression are at the top of her list. As a leader, she was also very honest, flexible, and very helpful. She was a type of woman who didn't let her title get in her head. She was very approachable and relatable. Although both Commissioner and Deputy moved forward while I was still working at the TDLWD, I can say I was impressed, honored, and thankful to earn the opportunity to work with them.

After leaving TDLWD, I discovered a puzzling situation. One of my coworkers, a gentle but sharp woman, is still not an administrator or at the least a director after twenty-six years of service to TDLWD. A few months ago, I learned that other staff members who are not able to match up to her expertise continued to get promoted ahead of her. I think there's something wrong with this picture.

This woman is a person that embodies humility, patience, and perseverance. Her knowledge of grants, fiscal compliance, policy, and technical assistance helped me understand my role as grants program manager. Unfortunately, her dedication and services to TDLWD are still being overlooked even after my departure in 2012. Despite being under-appreciated; she remains humbled and devoted to the Department and continues to contribute to the lives of Tennesseans through her work as an analyst. Besides my mother, I believe that I haven't met anyone quite as caring, gentle, and bright.

There are two lessons that I hope to teach here: First, the inequality and inability to embrace diversity in leadership is limiting and not something to be praised. I believe that a person should never be weighed by anything less than his or her ability, loyalty, and compassion for others regardless of a his or her age, race, or gender. I hope America will truly live up to the words of its Preamble. We as humans can treat our fellow humans better. We can use wisdom to love and to do the right thing, because it's the right thing to do. Doing so, we transcend our biases and preconceived notions. The second lesson is the importance of knowing which battles in life to stand up for. This can only be achieved by knowing one's own character, values, and circumstances.

I am also thankful that Deputy and Commissioner allowed me the opportunity to work at TDLWD. My broader knowledge of accounting, numerical analysis, financial management, contracts, procurement, transfer-modification of funds, and understanding of fiscal terminologies came from that experience.

When I was a staff of residence life at TSU, prior to the TDLWD job, I admired Dr. Michael Freeman, vice president of student affairs. He mentioned to me the importance of reading. He said once, "You have to read until you bleed." I don't know about the bleeding part, but I am glad Dr. Freeman pointed out the importance of reading. My TDLWD supervisor gave me a lot of work responsibilities and reading too.

However, there were several instances when I questioned if my TDLWD supervisor's motives towards me were good. I had mentioned to him that it would be cool for him to get promoted and to train me to take his place. He said I wasn't ready to be a director. Remember, I had managed facilities as a director at TSU before my new job at TDLWD. The TSU supervisor I had, before I became director, trained me as an RA, his assistant, and got me ready to take his place as director before he moved forward to higher and better roles with more responsibilities. I was hoping my TDLWD supervisor would do that too. However, my TDLWD supervisor tried to cut my salary. I fought it, and after having a meeting with human resources, my salary wasn't decreased. The ironic thing is he added responsibility after responsibility to my job description. I performed them to the best of my abilities. At the end of the day, I can say that my obstacles have always made me stronger and wiser. It got hard and very lonely at times in the furnace of life, and I condoned a few things that disappointed me. However, my inner peace, spirit to take initiative, and willingness to get things done overcame my challenges. There is more to this in chapter 11.

At twenty-nine years old, I pursued one of my career goals to add to my experience in the engineering technology and building construction fields. I linked up with a successful businessman, Don Hardin of Don Hardin Group, a construction management and project-engineering firm. Although Don didn't have a paid project for me, I met with him as a project apprentice on a weekly basis at 7:15 a.m. for about thirty minutes at the Turner Family Center construction site before I went to my government job around 8 a.m. I also went to the construction site on my own after work hours to learn everything I could about building a facility from the ground up. Don exposed me to the building construction world beyond just reading books.

I hope the reader has learned that patience, persistence, drive, and knowing your value are very important in the work environment. I also think it's important to stand up for yourself and advocate on behalf of those mistreated when there is a clear fact that inequality does exist. It cost me as you will learn in chapter 11. I do not regret doing it, because it also elevated me.

Chapter 10
A Deeper Foundation,
Furnace of Life – Nashville, TN

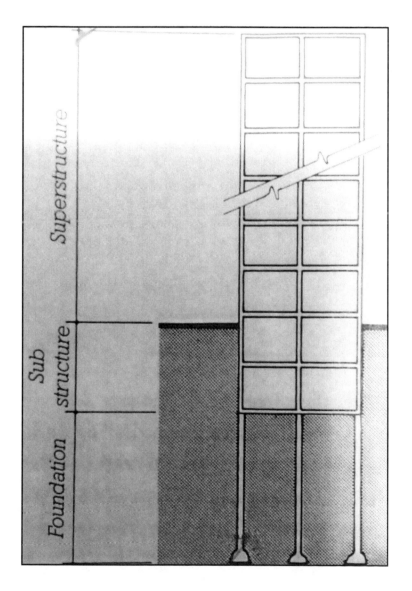

DON HARDIN GROUP offered me an apprentice role in one of my fields, building and construction. The project was the Turner Family Center. The frame is structural Steel and it had a lot of glass wall. The facility is used for assembling large and small groups. It is a multipurpose facility, 80000 square feet, green roof, LEED certified, silver. LEED is leadership in energy and environmental design. LEED aims to encourage builders and owners to build sustainably and invest resources in recycled building products, therefore helping the environment and mitigating building waste and pollution.

As I approached the Turner Family Center Construction site, I noticed that the excavation, wall footing, and slab-on-grade foundation had been constructed. I saw several plumbing pipes protruding from the earth, men looking at building plans, and a crane. For safety reasons, each item transported by a crane had a tag line to help direct the motion of the object being transported. Don Hardin pointed out the anchor bolts and the manholes on the north side of the site. He was happy that the structural steel columns arrived in a truck my first week with him on the construction site. The structural steel columns were connected to the anchor bolts. Some anchor bolts had four holes and others had more. A gusset plate connected the steel beams to the steel columns. Don asked me to point out the elevators' spaces to him.

I noticed two square spaces on the site with temporary lumber rails. I correctly pointed them out as the elevator spaces.

Don mentioned some workers on the site—ironworkers who specialized in the assembly and welding of steel frame structures. The four phases of design construction are conceptual, schematic, detail, and construction. In some instances, an architect prepared construction plans while a contractor priced what it would cost to build at different phases. Eventually, metal decking was placed on the second-floor beams. Don mentioned that the metal decking would be welded to the beams and then concrete would be poured on top. In addition, holes would be cut through the metal decking to allow plumbing lines to pass through. By the way, a fire watch person was present on the site always when welding took place. A fire watch person stays alert to make sure the construction site, workers, and the public are safe by preventing any hazards like fire.

At times, I went to the construction site on my own when Don was busy with other projects. Staircases were added to the southeast, southwest, and north sides of the building. After concrete was poured directly on the metal decking, a floater was used to level and smoothen the concrete. On the first level, concrete was also poured in the area for the kitchen. Don mentioned that a leveling tool helped workers gauge when to stop pouring concrete. The white pipes protruding from the ground were for sanitary use and cast iron (black) pipes were for grease. The orange objects on top of the steel rods were called *rebar caps*. The Turner Family Center was finished and turned out to be a beautiful building at Mehary Medical College in Nashville, Tennessee.

Chapter 11
CONFESSIONS,
FURNACE OF LIFE – NASHVILLE, TN

Hopefully, the reader is familiar with the 2002 movie *Antwone Fisher* starring Derek Luke, Denzel Washington, and Joy Bryant. At a young age, I experienced what an older woman did to Antwone sexually when he was a young boy in the foster home. This experience added to the reasons I distanced myself from women intimately for eighteen years straight, although I am and only attracted to women. It happened from the ages of ten to eleven. I didn't tell my grandmother that this woman molested me at a young age. Likewise, I didn't inform my mother until I was twenty-eight years old. I kept quiet for years due to shame and not even knowing how to start to tell. I'm sure there are many people out there who have experienced being molested by a relative (man or woman) as children. I advise you to not let fear, shame, or what people will think keep you from the necessary healing within. Carrying this experience around into adulthood can affect your interaction with family and friends, and it may even make you isolate yourself. Find someone you can trust to talk to, and let it go. Let out the shame, fear, hurt, and forgive the man or woman who violated you.

Parents and teachers, it is very important to keep a close eye on your children (or students) and even much more on family members, relatives, and friends that are around your children. Communicate with your children if they seem too quiet or distant. You may just be the one to stop a repeat molester or someone seeking to violate the innocence of your child or any child. It may be an uncle, an aunt, a cousin, a trusted family member, or a friend. Watch your children, please. Parents, if you do find out, it is important for the dignity of that child that you do not keep quiet. It's important to confront and report the molester. The thought that this may disgrace the family is nothing but fear and a lie. For the sake of complete healing for the victim, it's important to talk about it, prevent future attempts, and deal with the molester as you see proper. The bond between you and your child, and the safety of future children born into your family depends on it. I have forgiven the woman.

The combination of this experience, the physical and mental abuse that my mom experienced from my dad, and a desire to be like Paul the Apostle and not marry (which was stronger in high school and changed after I earned my engineering degree) contributed to the fact that I abstained from sex for so long.

I chose to become intimate by choice for the first time at age twenty-nine. The urge, pressure, and the fact that I had to prove to myself that I truly liked women were my excuses. I admit that my approach was not easy at all. There were several women attracted to me, but I didn't want to risk having a child and putting him or her through the pain my mom, my sister, and I experienced for so long. My dad was not present as a father and unfaithful as a husband. A child needs a loyal father and a wife needs a loyal husband. Likewise, a child needs a loyal mother and a husband needs a loyal wife. I have also realized that physical attraction and love are not the same. My mom is a very beautiful woman. However, her beauty didn't stop my dad from physically and mentally abusing her.

It is important to not base love or marriage on beauty, good looks, money, and physical attributes alone. Those things are important, but make sure to get to know someone's character, values, and likes or dislikes first. The friendship stage is very important. Building a relationship is like building a house. It's very important to have a solid foundation. When the house (relationship) is tested, it will last and not fall.

My dad tried to get involved in my life after I was already a man. By then, it was too late; I had already distanced myself from him. It was hard for me to embrace him. The resentment and dislike for him was so strong that I couldn't freely say "I love you, Dad" when he told me he loved me. I looked at action, not words. To me, he didn't understand the first thing about love. Love required commitment, loyalty, responsibility, and selflessness. Despite my dislike for him, my faith convinced me to visit him occasionally.

I pray to break the cycle of violence and disrespect against women. For me, there is a difference between a man and a male. I have forgiven my dad, but can never forget. Despite several attempts to heal the relationship and acting on the advice of elders to visit him in the past, he will not admit his mistakes. I can never honor that type of man. When a man is unwilling to admit to his mistakes and change his ways for better, it is difficult to honor or respect him.

My goal is to be a father to my future children, a good husband to my future wife, to be her best friend, and true companion. I constantly pray that God will heal the experience that my dad put my mom, sister, and me through. I have forgiven him too. I also must make sure as a man that I am truly ready for marriage and fatherhood. Even though I have the qualities for that right now, I'm not rushing it.

My experience with women had been good for the most part. Like I stated, I was very respectful and encouraged many women to have confidence in themselves, have high standards, and work towards their vision by setting goals. There were moments when some got too comfortable with me and wanted to get closer. Even though I wanted that too, I kept my guards up and never allowed it for many years. The combination of my life experience and not willing to be intimate in my early, mid, and late twenties was my Achilles heel. Why? A lot of women liked me, but I said no on many occasions (verbally and nonverbally). I didn't take advantage of the opportunity when some of those women wanted to be intimate. I'm sure my male friends are laughing right now. I don't regret this decision. It kept me from a lot of drama. It kept me strong, focused.

Almost-girlfriend One was a black, athletic, longhaired, funny lady with a cute accent. The funny thing is I was interested in one of her friends first, despite people telling me constantly she was attracted to me. The friend of Almost-girlfriend One and I just could not find time outside of work to hang out. Afterwards, I unwisely told the friend to forget I said I liked her. She was confused and disappointed, and I just thought, "let it go." Almost-girlfriend One and I were like best friends. We just clicked and enjoyed being around each other. I visited her apartment on occasion with my Alpha Phi Alpha bag (with snacks and drinks in it). We had cool conversations. She liked to laugh a lot and had a somewhat quick temper. Her physique would make an average man go crazy. I had self-control though. I met her mom once and she met my mom and a few relatives when I graduated in 2011 with my MPA degree.

My opportunity to be physically close with Almost-girlfriend One was clear one night I visited her. I prayed on my way too. I walked in. We had our usual cool conversation. After watching a movie with her, it got late. She showed no sign that she wanted me to go. I cleverly opened my computer and started telling her about my ideas and vision to engender a better Africa and Nigeria. If it wasn't for this clever move, that night would have went down in history as the night I was willing to be physically close the first time by choice. I guess I was still disturbed by my childhood experience and wasn't ready.

I kept my distance from Almost-girlfriend One after I resigned from the Department of Residence Life, a period when I thought I had an engineering job to transition to. I was dealing with a disappointment and I didn't communicate effectively with her. Prior to resigning, an engineering company had informed me that I would be called employed after graduating. I was not. It was one of the lowest points in my life. I was ashamed to tell her I was unemployed, and I called one day to inform her that I wasn't interested at the time. She was so disappointed. I felt bad. I later sent her a text message to tell her I desired to be with her eventually. We spoke occasionally on the phone, but I didn't put as much effort into communicating as I used to. I was more focused on getting employed again. I wasn't happy. We both lost interest.

Almost-girlfriend Two: I met both of her parents at church. I wasn't intimate with her either, although I recall a night we came close. There was a point when we both wanted to. My respect for her and her uncertain spirit influenced me to not take advantage of the opportunity. I was more of a friend and mentor to her. She was like a wave, constantly changing her mind about the possibility of us. My thought process was I would rather be with a woman with a stable mind. Her past relationships and experiences with being let down by men was like a disadvantage. When she finally met me, knowing that I would be faithful and caring, that I had a good job and would go to extreme lengths to make her happy, and that I kept it real with her, she couldn't grasp it. In her eyes, I was too good. She was afraid, maybe due to her past relationships. Therefore, I stopped pursuing her. Maya Angelou, in the movie *Medea's Family Reunion*, said, "Love is many things. One thing it is not and can never be is unsure." Almost-girlfriend Two had some good qualities though; she liked attending church, was caring, and liked to laugh. Her natural hair was also a plus.

At the age of twenty-nine, after letting go of Almost-girlfriend Two, I was partially disinterested in dating. At the same time, I started living recklessly. On one occasion, a policewoman gave me a ticket. At the time, I didn't see that she might have prevented me from a serious accident or injury to myself or someone else. A radical thing I did at that age was driving fast and recklessly (only when I was in the vehicle by myself). Thankfully, I wasn't involved in an accident. However, it was closing on me. Being given a ticket for driving in the emergency lane is a day I look back on and appreciate.

Prior to the ticket, I had a habit of driving in the emergency lane on few occasions to pass traffic. I knew that a police car could appear and I'd get a ticket for traffic violation. I didn't care. My mindset was what I had to do and where I had to be was more important. I needed to get to my destination ASAP, even if it meant breaking traffic laws and rules. It got so bad at one point. I was on my way home from work. The traffic was so backed up on I-40 West in Nashville; so I just decided to get on the right shoulder of the highway and drove (following an emergency truck on its way to help a stranded motorist).

I look back at this and shake my head. How did it get to that point? Why did I behave out of character? In a matter of days, I got a ticket for driving on an emergency lane again on my way to work. The truth is I knew better. I knew I was not supposed to drive on the emergency lane to pass traffic (despite how long traffic was). I was always in a hurry to get to work at that period in my life. I stopped the habit because I realized it was dangerous and could end up hurting someone or myself. I eventually decided it made more sense to give myself an extra fifteen, thirty, or forty-five minutes driving time in cities like Nashville with high traffic volume in the morning and after work. After attending traffic school, I watched a video. One thing was mentioned that day that prevented me from ever driving recklessly again. It was "Reckless drivers drive recklessly because they are not able to control some things in their lives."

That simple statement stayed with me. There were some things in life that I experienced, which held me back, and that I did not cause. The stress of these things triggered frustration. Therefore, when I was by myself in traffic at that period in life, the thoughts of being held back engendered a habit that could have led into an accident. I'm thankful it didn't and glad I stopped behaving out of character.

I eventually met Girlfriend 1 when I was twenty-nine. She was thirty years old when we met at a fraternity event in a restaurant located in West End neighborhood of Nashville, TN. The key thing about her was her honesty. We naturally had a good and long conversation the day we met. Something in me just wanted to be there for her. I encouraged her to let go of doubts regarding career aspirations and relationships. She told me she had been engaged in the past but didn't offer the specifics of why it ended. We just loved being around each other, with a bond that got stronger and stronger. We cared about each other. Our conversations were genuine. She cooked. Her smile was angelic and she deserved to be happy. She made me smile. She liked holding hands and loved cuddling a lot. We dated for two years and three months. More to come very soon regarding this relationship. In the meantime, I'd like to share significant events and activities during this same period.

A few months after meeting my girlfriend, I was elected president of Urban League Young Professionals of Middle TN (ULYPMT). Prior to the election, I was both the community and civic engagement chair for ULYPMT and the community service chair for Alpha Phi Alpha Fraternity, Inc. I served ULYPMT for a total of three years (about two years in the role of president). Something unexpected, shady, and unjust happened the day prior to my election as president of ULYPMT. Earlier that day at work (I worked at Tennessee Department of Labor and Workforce Development from 2012 to 2014), I had finished meeting with a second supervisor who agreed that I had done a job correctly by sending the necessary follow-up regarding a resource-sharing agreement for one of the thirteen Local Workforce Investment Areas we served. I eventually went back to my desk and immediately saw an email from an HR department head to come to his office. I left my desk and went. To my surprise, my second supervisor, who was just with me in his office less than three minutes prior, was also in the HR department head's office. I was handed a Notice of Separation.

Prior to the Notice of Separation and before I had a second TDLWD supervisor, I decided to communicate with my first TDLWD supervisor one day about the work environment and why so many qualified, high-performing employees were getting released. He didn't give me a genuine reason. My job responsibilities doubled immediately. I excelled at them anyway, despite my concerns. A few months after, my second TDLWD supervisor was brought in as my new supervisor, and my first TDLWD supervisor was promoted to assistant administrator.

Ladies and gentlemen, allow me to remind you that I wrote in chapter 9 (third to last paragraph) regarding my first TDLWD supervisor that there were many times I wondered if his motives towards me were good or bad. I mentioned to him before how it will be awesome for him to get a promotion and train me to take his current position as a director because I was once (for almost three years) due to being trained to be a director. I expected my first TDLWD supervisor to do the same, but he attempted to demote me from the Grants Program Manager role and cut my salary. I was professional about it, communicated with HR, kept my original position, and pay. He added more responsibilities to my role (without a pay increase). I performed those responsibilities as best as I could.

It eventually became clear that the HR department head, the workforce development administrator, my second TDLWD supervisor, and the new assistant workforce development administrator (my first TDLWD supervisor) were all working together to get rid of me. My first TDLWD supervisor and the workforce development administrator thought they were clever by using my second TDLWD supervisor and the HR department head as pawns to do their dirty work. What made it so disappointing was the pawns were new at their role, being used as a cover up, and African American. The HR department head got rid of a lot of African American employees after he was appointed to his new role. It was even more disturbing that the HR department head used this role and was being used to get rid of so much of his own. When I started the job in 2012, I was employed under the leadership of TDLWD Commissioner Karla Davis and Deputy Commissioner Elisa Malone (two strong black women, leading the entire TN Department of Labor and Workforce Development as I expounded upon in chapter 9). The fact was there were some administrators and directors of Caucasian descent that just could not stand the fact that they had to report to Commissioner and Deputy. Eventually both Commissioner and Deputy transitioned. Afterwards, the craziness, racism, and prejudice I witnessed firsthand in a state government agency made me very uncomfortable. The governor of Tennessee at the time eventually appointed a new commissioner, who happened to be a Caucasian male.

Anyway, the true intentions of the so-called new leadership of TDLWD came to light even more. Many African American directors, managers, and assistant administrators who were employees before Commissioner and Deputy transitioned were fired at an alarming rate. It got so bad that I had to start asking questions in such a racist and prejudiced work environment. If anyone reading this book has question about my statements or questions their validity, please go to the Tennessee Department of Labor and Workforce Development. Ask for data on those employees that were released between early 2013 and mid 2014 (pay attention to the percentage and number of African Americans released and you will have your answer). If TDLWD HR is hesitant to provide this data or if the data seems incomplete, please ask the United States Department of Labor for it. I hope States are required to send a report on a yearly basis to the federal government regarding this type of data to help keep the states accountable when it comes to diversity and inclusion.

That day I was released happened to be the day I also had to communicate my platform (as an aspiring president) to Urban League Young Professionals of Middle TN members. After informing my girlfriend about what happened at work, my focus immediately shifted to preparation for my speech. I did not say a word regarding being released unjustly to the ULYPMT membership that night. My speech was powerful, full of passion, mixed emotions, and very precise on what I would do as president (a non-paying role that's more like a job by the way). I was so upbeat, but no one could tell I was also hurting inside. I had to be strong. I had to overcome the bullshit, racism, prejudice, countless rejections, injustice, and obstacles. Members and leaders approached me to run for president, and I didn't want to let them down because I just lost my job. Dr. Martin Luther King Jr. once said, "The ultimate measure of a man is not where he stands in times of comfort and convenience, but where he stands at times of challenge and controversy." To me, losing a job I worked so hard at was one of those many unjust tests I experienced in the furnace of life.

Simisola, my sister, had relocated to Washington, D.C. by this time. She worked at the Tennessee Department of Labor and Workforce Development. She was released several months before. I informed her about losing my job and my intention to fight the injustice. She advised me to speak with Commissioner Davis; so, I did. Commissioner knew I was very angry, and I informed her about my intention to confront the injustice. I was advised by her to pick my battles wisely even if it was true that a clear injustice was done. She advised me to move on. That advice was not what I expected. I already had letters prepared, a general plan in place, and an intention to go to local news to raise awareness on the racism and prejudice that was taking place. Something in me took heed of her counsel because I trusted her, still do, and she was like a mentor when it came to career advice for my sister and me.

There is a saying that life has a way of shaming your enemies. I believe so. Why? My sister eventually was hired by the U.S. Department of Labor after being released from the Tennessee Department of Labor. She is now working in D.C. and manages the same program at a federal level. I will share how the same enemies were shamed when it came to me very soon, even though it took one year and six months to get another full-time job. Yes, I had started a side business of providing building floor plans at this time. However, revenue wasn't continuously flowing. I woke up sometimes feeling defeated. I felt like a failure because, once again, I didn't have a paying full-time job in any of my fields. My savings tremendously decreased. However, I didn't quit. It's just not in my spirit or blood to give up. I had to be strong. Eric Thomas, an inspirational speaker, once confirmed to me , "You're already in pain. Don't quit now. Get a reward for it." This had been my mind set since day one, no matter what.

Let me quickly state here that it was a privilege to serve and lead ULYPMT and the team was awesome. We made things happen. We were young professionals who cared about the Nashville community and took initiative to make lives a little bit better for all in the areas of jobs, healthy lifestyle, education, housing affordability, and youth advocacy. Our parent organization was Urban League of Middle TN (ULMT), which was under the leadership of the awesome and active CEO Patricia Stokes. The mission of the National Urban League (founded in 1910) and ULMT is to enable African Americans, other minorities, and disenfranchised groups to secure economic self-reliance, power, parity, and civil rights. The 2014-2016 Urban League Young Professionals of Middle TN executive committee made a strong impression on me, and I do appreciate their time and efforts.

Although I learned a lot about women from my girlfriend, I admit that I broke up with her on two occasions, which was never my intention starting out. I still find it difficult that I caused a woman I cared about to cry because I said I wasn't sure about us. It is still shocking because I am well known for encouraging women, making them laugh, and treating them like sisters. This was not a typical breakup. The first lasted a few hours with back and forth text messages. The second lasted a few months and we remained faithful to each other. She was ready to get married and I wasn't. Was it because she was my first girlfriend and I wasn't her first boyfriend? Was it because I just wanted to make sure she was the one for me? Was it because of my career aspirations, vision, and other life goals that kept me from settling down with a woman who was ready to follow me anywhere? At times, I wondered if I should have married her when she was ready?

The fact is we both helped each other when times were good and bad. We helped each other financially, spiritually, and intellectually; we were like best friends. At the time, I felt like I wasn't successful enough, had personal career goals to realize, and didn't want to let a relationship take away that hunger. I wasn't ready for marriage and children, even though I desired those things. We had so much fun together. My heart, after we communicated about my concerns leading to breaking up the second time, just went right back to her. Eventually I had to leave Nashville to another state because I got a new job. I tried many times to stay in Nashville. I wanted to stay there because I had lived there for around twenty years. It was a second home and I met so many cool people. My network in Nashville, TN is huge and I was blessed to have significant influence there. However, one of the two career field I desired was available at another State.

I informed my girlfriend, and we both knew it might be the end of the relationship. I gave her my address and the thought of her coming with me entered my mind. I also knew that meant (for her) leaving her job to find another one, which would take time and require breaking her lease. The morning I left, I was sad and she was very sad too. We spoke a few times on phone after I left, but our communication wasn't what it used to be. Close to five months after I left Nashville, I finally had the peace of mind to keep my word. I had informed her in the early stages of the relationship that I would marry her, and she wanted to marry me. When I called her to tell her I was ready to marry her, she was no longer sure. She didn't say no and didn't say yes. She did say that when she was ready—when she communicated that she desired to be my wife and would have done anything to support me (like moving with me when I left)—I had made her felt like she wasn't good enough.

I communicated with her that I was not ready at the time she desired to marry me, due to putting career goals as first priority. After researching my new job, I knew I also needed to make sure I could perform the duties and get my feet on the ground. I had limited information on what I'd be doing during the transition. I just knew it required the best of the best. At times, I wondered if I was selfish for putting career aspirations before marriage at the time? The lesson I learned from that relationship was I should never take for granted a woman's unconditional love and support. I should have married her at the time she was ready to marry me. If two people truly liked and loved each other and both helped each other in good and bad times, go ahead with marriage.

Yes, I made three more attempts to communicate with her about being ready to marry her and explained why I approached our relationship the way I mentioned. I even wrote her sister-in-law and asked her to help communicate my intentions to her brother and help me beg her. We did speak on those three occasions on the phone. She gave me the same reply above regarding not being sure and that I had made her feel she wasn't good enough.

A few weeks later, I flew to Nashville on October 2016 to communicate with her in person and attempt to convince her for the last time. It also happened to be TSU's homecoming 2016. I also was there to take care of a few things regarding this book. I had to see her because it didn't make sense to me that she was no longer sure about us getting married. This was what she had always and earnestly desired, communicated, and worked towards for two years and a few months, and here she was now granted with peace of mind on a golden platter. When we met at the Opry Mills Mall in Nashville, I asked her three important questions: Can you explain further what you meant by I made you feel like you were not good enough? Do you realize that our breakups didn't last that long? Why are you throwing away what you said were the happiest moments of your life?

First, she replied that although my actions showed I cared about and loved her, I didn't say it enough with words. Second, she also agreed that our breakups weren't the typical break ups. Finally, she wanted me to move on without her. I still think she wasn't sure or was afraid, or maybe she was in a new relationship or it was something else she wasn't comfortable telling me. Anyway, I do wish her the best. After my visit in Nashville, I had to let it go with peace of mind. My final attempt was the Nashville visit. I pray and know I will find my queen and wife eventually.

Chapter 12
FAITH AND POLITICS,
FURNACE OF LIFE – NASHVILLE, TN

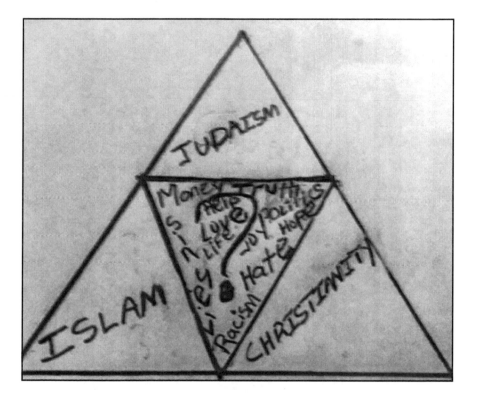

On June 12, 2016, I woke up to CNN reporting a hate crime that had claimed the lives of fifty people and injured many more in Orlando, Florida. This crime targeted gay people at a nightclub. I was in a state of silence for about twelve hours that day. I empathized with the victims and their family members. Afterwards, President Obama gave a national speech regarding the mass murder. I sensed his weary heart. Why? That moment marked the fifteenth time during his presidency addressing the senseless murder of people either at a place of worship, a school, or a public gathering. These crimes gained national attention. President Obama usually requested the United States Congress to support his call to action and help draft responsible bills to mitigate gun violence in the U.S.

Unfortunately, at the time, getting some leaders in the legislative branch to support the president's request on common sense gun laws to protect American citizens was difficult. There is a saying that a nation divided cannot stand. Any nation where constant tolerance of any major political groups, lobbyists, organization, or party that focuses more on political and monetary gains than protecting all people can never come to a solution on issues like gun violence. It is up to the citizens of that nation to remove those illegitimate leaders if they do not act to protect all citizens, especially when lives are involved.

Sometimes I wondered if some of the members of the Grand Ol' Party (GOP; Republican Party) just couldn't stand the fact that a black man (Barack Obama) was the president of a powerful nation like the U.S. ? Were they so blinded by their racism and prejudice that they couldn't collaborate with the president on common sense laws that will save lives?

I eventually posted a message on Facebook that day to share what was on my mind regarding the hate crime in Orlando. I said, in part, that despite faith, sexual orientation, or upbringing, remember we all had life experiences growing up. It's better to understand people's pain or upbringing first and not be so quick to judge. Islam, Christianity, Judaism, Hinduism, Buddhism, just to name a few, do not support extremist acts that use faith as a reason to take a life or lives. This mindset is evil at its core, masquerading as faith. Any faith should seek to preserve lives, not take them. Love, not hate.

I still remember the words of my grandmother. While I was still in Nigeria, she said, "Your mother wants you to start practicing Christianity." My grandmother, a devoted Muslim and the one responsible for my, my sister's, and my cousins' Muslim background, showed no objection to my mother's request. The fact is, I grew up going to mosques to pray and observed the Muslim holidays constantly. My full birth name is Abayomi Oluwaseun Abdul-Majid Samuel Atolagbe. Samuel is my Christian name and the Abdul-Majid is my Muslim name. I came from an extended family of both Christians and Muslims.

Life has humbled and enlightened me to the point that I can coexist with and love anyone from any faith. The Muslims believe in Allah, the creator whom the Christians refer to as God. Jews refer to God as Yahweh. Muslims do not refer to Christ as the son of God. They refer to Christ as a holy man or prophet. I will also say radical Islam is a word made up by the media and news stations. True Islam (Muslims) cares about humanity. How do I know? I know because I grew up in Lagos, Nigeria. It is full of true Muslims and true Christians. I know for sure the thought of destroying each other was not in our minds.

Extremists of any faith do that. Any idea, person, group, or country that mistreats, hurts, denies equal privileges, or goes to the extreme to kill people who do not agree with its ideals has evil at its core.

I had my share of struggles when it came to faith. Maybe I was just going through phases or maybe I wasn't content with having genuine faith alone. Isn't there supposed to be something more, for genuine sons and daughters of God, if the Bible is taken literally? For example, I would rather operate beyond the earthly realm to help restore joy to the hurting, health to the sick, sight to the blind, freedom to those in bondage, order to disorder, and solutions to life struggles. I just don't want to pretend or mislead those who are hurting, in pain, broken, lost, and helpless like some faith leaders do these days. I am not interested and will never be interested in misleading people. I am also not in a rush at all to lead a church. I'm not interested in being a pastor unless God directly reveals this to me and equips me. People need real solutions. I have always desired for God to show me his glory and anoint me for his kingdom (the type of anointing exemplified by biblical icons like Moses, Paul, Joseph, Samson, Job, Peter, and the prophets). Only time will tell. I don't go to church as much lately. Why, you may ask? The true answer is my life experiences that I shared in previous chapters, as well as some unanswered questions. The fact that slave owners historically used faith or the bible to validate slavery is also a factor.

It eventually got to a point in my life where I started asking key questions: Why did God put the tree of knowledge of good and evil in the Garden of Eden, knowing that both Eve and Adam would disobey? Who created God? Is God willing to forgive Satan as God required us to forgive our enemies? Why was the bible changed so much throughout history and why have there been so many versions and interpretations throughout history?

I still remember a time I informed my mom at a young age that I desired to be like the Apostle Paul, be celibate, and not get married. I just desired to please God so much and was willing to do anything and go anywhere God lead me. I was on fire for God. I was passionate as it gets and was willing to do about anything to hear God himself speak to me as he did to Joseph, Moses, and Abraham in the biblical days. I loved God.

To conclude, I have seen people experience so much pain and loss, have experienced critical moments where God kept silent, and felt like God left me hanging when I really needed an intervention. Despite those disappointments, I still followed God for many years. Anyway, it reached a point where I decided that if God desired my heart, God needed to act. No amount of preaching, going to church, or reading the Bible was enough to retain the zeal for God I once had. I could see through people (both believers and nonbelievers). I could feel their pain, hurt, confusion, and deception. Most churches, in all honesty, are limited and powerless when it comes to real solutions or confronting spirits or evil beyond the earthly realm. We live in a world where evil and injustice prevail and megachurches continue to be built at alarming rate. However, little has been done to bring about positive solutions to key problems (racism, economic inequity, housing disparities, inadequate education, health issues, and violence of all kinds).

Life just made me re-examine things and seek truth. My heart became seared. It came to a stage where words were just not enough. Only action by God and the hand of God would do. I don't pray as much as I used to. However, I still do pray for my family, people, nations, and myself. I give thanks much more than I pray. I like saying the Lord's Prayer, Psalm 1, Psalm 23, and the Prayer of Jabez:

"Jabez cried out to the God of Israel, 'Oh, that you would bless me and enlarge my territory! Let your hand be with me, and keep me from harm so that I will be free from pain' and God granted his request." (1 Chronicles 4.10, NIV version)

Deep inside my heart, I still seek truth. That passion still burns within, but only now from a lens of reality. The full truth comes not from man, and any man that claims to know it all is a liar and a deceiver.

Chapter 13
THE BUSINESS OWNER
AND A FEDERAL EMPLOYEE, FURNACE OF LIFE –
UNITED STATES (DMV AREA- NORTH EAST)

It took me close to half a day to get to the DMV area (D.C.-Maryland-Virginia) from Nashville in my truck. The cool things during the road travel were the mountains, hills, lands and farms covered with trees for many miles, and the sense of nature was cool. After spending about twenty years in Nashville, I relocated in March of 2016 to the DMV area.

The view of my new place, when on the patio, is breath taking. It caused me to pause and think about nature, its fullness, and appreciate creation much more. I often found myself gazing at the sky for miles until my eyes meet the horizon. I do miss Nashville, TN. I met so many cool, intelligent, driven, like-minded, and beautiful people there. My mother and some of my relatives still reside in Nashville. My network and influence there is very strong, full of state and local leaders, corporate leaders, fraternity brothers, driven young professionals, genuine friends, and real people from different types of backgrounds I have been bless to know since the mid 90s until I left in March 2016.

Although I am thankful for my full-time job with the federal government, I wish I were in Nashville instead (working for the same federal government). Home is where the heart is. I have two homes: Nigeria and Nashville. I also have the spirit of an eagle that is always prepared to soar to new heights, even if it requires a new place in life.

In chapter 8, I mentioned that I started a business of providing building floor plans and had some clients in Nashville. I just went public with the company MoorTECH after relocating. I am also licensed to provide internet cabling for homes and commercial buildings. The disadvantage with being currently new in the DMV area is building my client base from ground zero (not knowing anyone or business connects). I do believe that things will get better businesswise. Things like that are normal. A businessman or businesswoman knows exactly what I am talking about. The question of why I left Nashville might arise with the reader. I tried hard to stay there. I have two passions, interconnected to my ultimate vision of using my talents, strengths, and skills to help make lives a little bit better for people. I don't know if this will require moving to Nigeria, staying here in the U.S. and moving to another big city, staying in DMV area, or moving back to Nashville. Only time will tell. In addition to my company and full-time job, I also have a part-time job. We service interactive devices like cell phones, laptops, cameras, tablets, and many other home electronic, entertainment, and computer-based devices.

Anyway, I have been putting the work in (on my hustle and grind). No excuses. Starting a business requires calculated risk, investing a lot of time and resources, and undying persistence. It requires tough skin and humble confidence in times of progress. To make all this work, I currently work the night shift as a federal employee so I can have the time to take care of business during the day. I just love creating, building, and making things work using engineering principles and technology. It's who I am. It defines me. It's my hobby and my passion. I have little time for social activities but also understand I need to find that balance. I am thankful and believe I will soon achieve other important goals like marriage, a happy home, fatherhood, and loyalty as a husband and best friend to my future wife-queen.

Chapter 14
THE VISIT TO LAGOS ISLAND, FURNACE OF LIFE – NIGERIA

ABOUT TWENTY YEARS after moving from my birth country, Nigeria, with my mother and sister in 1996, I went back to visit. The plane left from Washington, D.C. in the middle of October 2016 and returned the first week of November 2016. Although my mother, sister, and I communicated with family members often and just one of my uncles, his children, and wife traveled to the U.S. to visit us, not seeing most of my relatives for about twenty years was a very long time. I came from a very big family full of Muslims and Christians, with a lot of relatives. I love my culture, although I dislike a few things about it I will share. I'm very proud to be a Nigerian. I like my heritage. I almost didn't visit Nigeria due to my new job. However, my sister wanted me to go. I was also convinced by a co-worker to go. So I persisted, and the two people I report to at my job eventually made it possible for me to visit Nigeria.

The plane departed from D.C., stopping briefly in France. Then it finally left France for Nigeria. Flight time was long, but worth it. I arrived at Murtala Airport in Lagos, Nigeria. As soon as the plane landed, I knew I was in Nigeria because of the outdoor heat. When I exited the Murtala airport, my uncle eventually arrived to pick me up in his car. My grandmother, although now old, was still sharp despite limited mobility. She saw me and I saw her saying my name. She was shocked. She probably thought it was a dream. My mother had visited

Nigeria two times prior to, but the fact that I came this time was both a blessing and honor for her.

I also made sure to visit and study the social, living, road, commercial, and economic conditions of all the places I visited in Nigeria, from Lagos Island where I was born to surrounding areas I recognized or had attended school like to Ibadan where my mother also worked and resided at one point. I also visited Songo Ota, Ikeja, Ikoyi, Victoria Island, Ikorodu, Ilorin, and more. I had fun during my visit and I also made sure to make it count. I am a man of purpose, balanced with fun. I desired to see and study in person what I had read and heard for years regarding the divide between the wealthy and poor in Nigeria. Lagos is a very good example of a country where there isn't enough of a middle class compared to the wealthy or rich. This isn't helping the country. Many poor people continue to suffer beyond most imagination. I think the larger a middle class any country has, the easier most of the people living in that country can afford needs like a home, a car, clothes, and food. Unfortunately, Nigeria is not there yet.

I believe in a type of government and nation where the middle class is the majority and poor people can rise economically. It allows and closes the gap between the wealthy and poor. It will require a non-corrupt government and for most the citizens to demand good leadership. Citizens must also be good stewards of their environment and help bring order to it. The poor have a better chance to be successful and to be able to afford necessities like food, clothing, shelter, transportation, and health care with this form of governance, approach, and economics.

During my visit in Lagos, I saw what I already knew. The poor areas and markets were very overcrowded. The heat doesn't help either for those who walk or rely on overcrowded, unsafe, or outdated public buses, bikes, tricycles, and cars to get to work. The poor cannot afford what the wealthy in Nigeria can. These things are the comfortable, big, luxurious houses, jets, mansions, cars, and guards. I did see that Nigeria had a blue bus route. However, a small percentage could afford this alternative public transportation. In Lagos, people are either wealthy or poor; the middle class is very small.

Nigeria has a lot of resources, like intelligence, land, culture, wealth, creativity, and technology, but what disturbs me is its weakness. A lot of its leaders are corrupt. The current president, Mahammadu Buhari, stated he is fighting this corruption. I also learned there was a period when 80 kobo equaled 1 American dollar in the early 1980s. By the way, 100 kobo equals 1 Niara in the Nigerian economy. In other words, the Nigerian economy used to be much stronger than the U.S.'s economy. Now in 2016, 1 dollar can be exchanged for about 308 Naira to 420 Naira, depending on if the exchange takes place at a bank, a legit foreign exchange business, or underground exchange places. The corruption has been going on for years. Some Nigerians have given up, accepted it as the norm, and are less hopeful. President Buhari stated he is currently fighting one of the roots of this problem: the judicial branch in Nigeria.

A nation like Nigeria where corrupt leaders can bribe the judge with money, who then rules in favor of these corrupted leaders, is out of order. A nation like Nigeria where some of the elected officials each have ten to twenty luxurious vehicles, jets, and many houses; continue to embezzle money, opening foreign bank accounts; and build houses in other nations to flee justice if it comes is out of order. They steal the money and revenues that are supposed to be used to repair bad commercial and residential roads and bridges, create jobs for the college graduates, and train the unemployed to attain new skills to become employable. A nation like Nigeria where the greed of its government continues to make it impossible for a lot of its citizens to afford basic needs (healthy food, adequate housing, clothing, vehicles) is out of order. A nation like Nigeria where some Nigerian police collect bribes from those visiting and even its own citizens is out of order. A nation like Nigeria that barely enforces traffic laws and where there is so much noise from overcrowded public and private transportation, depending on the area, is out of order.

As the past and late president of Nigeria, Umaru Musa Yar' Adua, once said, "A nation where illiteracy and disregard for law and order is constantly tolerated and celebrated cannot stand." I will add that a nation like Nigeria where some elected officials running for re-election use stolen money to bribe some desperate citizens in return for votes is out of order. A nation like Nigeria where noisy generators are the major source of electricity in some areas and those that cannot afford it are at the mercy of the electric company that doesn't provide daily electricity is out of order. A nation like Nigerian where hate between tribes exists and evildoers (witches and wizards) hurt and take lives of the innocent for the sake of money, power, and greed is out of order.

I love my two homes: Nigeria and the U.S. As far as Nigeria, we can do better. I like the culture. The food, the beauty, the discipline, the people, the sense of fashion, helpful traditions, the creativity, and our intelligence is second to none. We rank highest when it comes to academic acumen abroad. Our young citizens and students who travel abroad for education excel in math, English, writing, trigonometry, science, geometry, numbers, calculus, Latin, Greek, etc. In fact, Nigeria alone has over four hundred languages, and it's growing. There is no subject in which Nigerians lack proficiency or even mastery. We are well educated. We lead our classes after graduations. We are builders, and our ancestors are alchemists, astronomers, inventors, inventors, leaders, queens, kings, and an envy of the world at a time prior to the corruption.

Nigerians, these corrupted leaders must go at all cost if they insist on their ways. Keep them accountable. Be brave and demand better from the government. Children are the future and they deserve better environment and education, and the young men and women deserve jobs after graduation. Put them to work and pay them a fair wage to repair the damage that has been done. I ask the Nigerian government to please consider the future of Nigeria and its young men and women. They will produce the future sons and daughters of Nigeria. They will be the future fathers, mothers, leaders, parents, doctors, nurses, teachers, leaders, engineers, bankers, lawyers, government officials, police officers, entertainers, writers, and faith leaders. I ask the Nigerian government to understand the urgency of creating jobs for them after graduation.

In any country (including Nigeria and the U.S.A.), a young woman should not have to be a prostitute or a servant to be able to make the money needed to take care of herself and her loved ones, or to be able to afford necessary things like food, clothing, and shelter. Any government that does not mitigate this epidemic has failed its people. A young man should not have to be a gang member, thief, dope dealer, or a thug to be able to provide for his family. Remember, the way of the wicked will eventually perish. The truth eventually will be unveiled no matter the extremes taken by wicked and greedy leaders to cover it up.

During my visit in Lagos, I was fortunate to see much nicer places too, like Ikeja, Victoria Island, Ikoyi, etc. However, I still believe that the true worth or greatness of a nation depends on the living, health, and economic conditions of a greater percentage of its citizens. President of United States Barack Obama said,

Making your mark on the world is hard. If it were easy, everybody would do it. But it's not. It takes patience, it takes commitment, and it comes with plenty of failure along the way. The real test is not whether you avoid this failure, because you won't. It's whether you let it harden or shame you into inaction, or whether you learn from it; whether you choose to persevere.

The future relies now on choice. As Nigerians or any nation for that matter with similar circumstance, let us do better.

Epilogue
FIRE AND WATER, FURNACE OF LIFE: FROM NIGERIA TO AMERICA

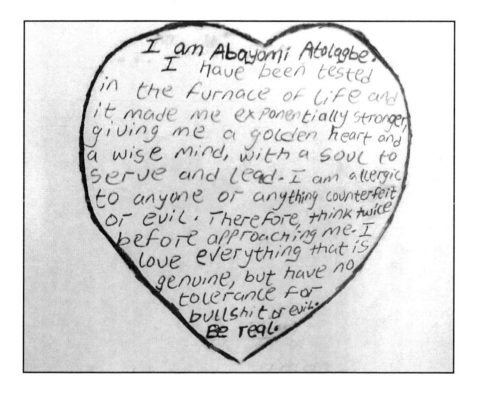

LADIES AND GENTLEMEN, going through the furnace is beyond the bad thing it may seem and feel at first. In fact, it is meant to make us stronger (mind, body, and soul) for those who decide to not give up. Remember, you have the power within you to overcome life obstacles. The furnace of life neither made me good nor bad. It made me real, very resilient, and resourceful. Never give up. Obstacles are inevitable in life. They help make us stronger, better, and successful. They provide the needed foundation and ability to last. If you like, love, and are very good at something, go get it! Embrace obstacles, because it's usually when things you aspire to achieve are hardest to attain that you must not give up. This approach makes all the difference and can lead you to attain exactly what you desire or even much more. Use the obstacle as an opportunity, keep pushing, and give it your all. It will be worth it if you do and persevere.

It leads to joy and makes you more relatable, real. Some obstacles can seem impossible to overcome at times, but can be overcome. It starts with believing in yourself, no matter how many people don't believe in you. It's a matter of the heart. It's not about how big or small, how rich or poor, or how educated or uneducated you are. Please, believe in yourself and act. You can win. Ask for help. There is no shame in it. Know who your true friends are. You will know them by their actions, not words. It doesn't matter how bad the situation is or how long it takes—believe and act. Anything is possible. Your situation can get better, no matter how hopeless it may seem at first. Surround yourself with those who will uplift you, challenge you because they love you, and help you be a better version of yourself (mind, body, and soul). Be aware of frienemies. They are those who claim to be your friend but don't desire for you to progress.

Jesus Christ mentioned in his teachings that no one is good or perfect, not even one. We all have flaws, but the key is to not let that flaw be a limitation to success in life, career, faith, and family. The key is being real with each other in words and actions. Never use a flaw as an excuse or a justification for selfish motives. Honesty in the present prevents hurt, pain, confusion, hatred, and evil in the future. Get to know people's pain, early life struggles, and character first despite the color of the skin.

Those who choose faith and the heart follow the path of water. Those who choose action and the mind follow the path of fire. I believe we need both. In my life, furnace represents my obstacles and life represents my choices to stay alive, persevere, and overcome. In other words, I had to use water (heart and faith) and fire (my mind and action) to rise above my life obstacles in both Nigeria and America. I had to go through the furnace of life, a necessary path. It is beyond me. It is also about the people who will be affected by the choices I constantly make in life, career, and business. It has all made me credible. I have learned from going through the furnace about not quitting, the importance of choices, the importance of keeping my word, and how everything I say and do affects others. It helped me, and I hope it will positively help those who read this book. The investment, time, and years spent on the book was for you. It is beyond me. This makes it worth it to go through the furnace of life.

I've been tested in the furnace of life, and it only made me exponentially stronger, giving me a golden heart, a wise mind, and a soul to serve. I am allergic to anyone or anything counterfeit or evil. I love everything that's genuine, but have zero tolerance for evil, ill motives and intent, deceivers, deception, and ignoble impulses.

In the foreword for this book, I shared a poem, "House of Alpha," by Sydney P. Brown. Poetry and poems are part of the things I do and read to keep me engaged in the furnace of life. Other poems I recommend are "If" by Rudyard Kipling, "Invictus" by William Ernest Henley, "The Test of a Man" (author unknown), "Our Deepest Fear" by Marianne Williamson, and "Don't Quit" (author unknown).

I hope I have taken the reader on a journey of time well spent regarding my experiences so far in Nigeria and America. I am glad and thankful I have been blessed with a spirit to persevere. I sometimes look back and wonder how I was able to cope with countless obstacles and rejections. What made it impossible was the more I tried, the more I encountered obstacles. I stopped counting short of a thousand rejections during my career journey. However, I never quit nor gave up. I kept pushing. That made all the difference, leading to the triumphs and successes I had. A man who doesn't work doesn't eat. I hustle and grind constantly (true grit). Exercise kept me alive literally, no joke. Without it, I would have been very ill, unhealthy, or maybe worse. Exercise was my time out from the furnace. I am thankful for my training ground, the hard-knock life, lessons about true manhood, and the strong foundation attained in the furnace. I have no shame about my confessions; I've learned from it, and I'm thankful my childhood mistakes never turned into habits. Glad I stopped very early. For that, I have been blessed and have been trusted in my life and career experiences to manage and keep sensitive and private information, including money and resources; I do not misuse them.

Now that I have finished this book, my passion, desires, and zeal to help make people's lives better has been rekindled and made even stronger, and I hope God will guide me with the wisdom, knowledge, and understanding on how to do more. I am passionate about engineering and government. About twenty years later after leaving Lagos, Nigeria, for the United States of America, I visited my birth country for the very first time and finished the manuscript for the book there. I didn't plan it this way. This is not coincidence, it is Providence. Because there is evil in this world, I believe with all my heart that good also exists and always conquers evil. It's a matter of time. Despite my questions for God, I can say the key principle and the golden rule behind any true faith is to love (regardless of color or beliefs). Any religion or legalistic idea that does otherwise is false. Likewise, anyone or group that takes the word of the creator (God, Allah, Yahweh, and other names attributed to a higher power) out of context is evil and self-motivated, not faith inspired. Faith never and can never be justified as reason to kill, hurt, discriminate, and look down on another human being. Anyone or group that does this in the name of any faith is evil, self-motivated, and false. It is better to know and understand a fellow human first for his or her character, not by preconceived notions learned from home.

Dr. Martin Luther King Jr. once said he had a dream of a world where we will be judged not by the color of our skin but by the content of our character. This makes sense. I hope humans will realize this dream soon. Skin color doesn't matter. Let us treat each other better regardless of skin color. Racism is nothing but fear, and it is taught. It also limits the racist. The creator never made a mistake. The fact that some humans and other living things are considered black, some considered white, and some are considered a variety of both colors is a label. It is the character of that label that matters. I wish there was no label when it comes to humans. The creator is not boring, not narrow minded, and not one dimensional as some people may think. Creation confirms that color is the quintessence, the perfect example of creativity and class.

Remember: Don't quit. I'm available for conversations as time permits. I'd like to learn from you too. Most importantly, you are powerful beyond measure. And remember to be a thermostat. Cool situations, life, and environment down when it's hostile (hot) and bring warmth when it's dangerous (cold). It requires honesty, bravery, knowledge, understanding, and prudence. Ask questions if you don't know. There's no shame in it. Leaders ask questions. Stay humble and embrace the process. It gets better—and remember to enjoy life to the fullest :)

CPSIA information can be obtained
at www.ICGtesting.com
Printed in the USA
LVOW11s1137010317
525598LV00001BA/1/P